STORYTELLING
THE PRESENTER'S SECRET WEAPON

JOHN CLARE

By the same author:

Communicating Clearly about Science and Medicine

The 7 Deadly Sins of Scientific Presentations (and how to avoid them)

John Clare's Guide to Media Handling

Patents, Patients and Profits – Media Reporting of the Pharmaceutical Industry

Organ Farm (with Jenny Bryan): Modern Miracle or Genetic Time Bomb?

First Printing: 2018.

Paperback ISBN: 978-1-78955-235-5

Ebook ISBN: 978-1-78955-236-2

For information about special discounts for bulk purchases, foreign and subsidiary rights, please contact story@lionsdenpublishing.com

Published by LionsDen Publishing Ltd.
Boundary House   Boston Road   London   W7 2QE

Cover Design: Red Raven Book Design

Interior Design: Red Raven Book Design

Printed in the UK

TABLE OF CONTENTS

ACKNOWLEDGEMENTS

It has been said that an author never really finishes a book, but eventually someone takes it from them and says 'That's enough now. It's done.' That's how I have felt writing this one. It's culled from all the experience and expertise I have gathered over the past 25 years as a communication and presentation coach.

I've acquired that information from so many people. They include friends, colleagues, clients and some of the thousands of presenters I've worked with or seen at conferences all over the world. It's been a privilege to work with so many creative people who, although very different personalities, have one thing in common - they're all great communicators.

Many of them have been colleagues at LionsDen Communications with whom I've shared stages, conference rooms and airport lounges. They know who they are and it would be impossible to list them all here.

However, I owe a special debt of gratitude to my wife, Maxine Mawhinney, who inspires me in everything I do, and my children Dan, Ollie and India, all of whom have grown into hugely supportive influences and constructive critics.

INTRODUCTION

Think about the presentations you've seen that are truly memorable. Those with a clear message delivered in an engaging way. Presented by someone who's made the subject interesting, knows why you're there and understands what you need to know. Someone who, while clearly an expert, talks in language you understand and illustrates their key points with clear examples. The kind of person who's so good at presenting, and so engaging, they seem to have a secret weapon. They do. It's called *storytelling*.

Hold on a minute. *Storytelling? Isn't that just for kindergartens, campfires and kids' bedtime?* That's a common response when I tell people I teach storytelling to business people for a living. It's understandable - after all, the word 'story' has a soft, off-duty feel to it. Fairy stories, ghost stories, bible stories, Aesop's Fables...all fine and a bit of fun for kids and young people, but we're adults, doing serious jobs. We need to make serious points, with hard facts delivered in a serious manner...and that's how it's always been. So we'll just stay with our PowerPoint slides, bullet points, org charts, flow diagrams and laser pointers, thank you. If it takes effort for people to digest the key points, that's fine. Nobody said it was going to be easy. We're in the business of information, and the facts are what matter. Right?

Not entirely. Of course the facts, data or information are the point of most business presentations, and only a fool would argue otherwise. However, the way you *deliver* that information has a big impact on how much of it people retain. Think again about the types of stories I mentioned earlier. What do you remember from The Bible? The story of the Good Samaritan? The Prodigal

Son? The Sower? These are all parables, or stories with a moral point. Think of Aesop's Fables...what do you remember? The boy who cried wolf? The goose that laid golden eggs? The tortoise and the hare? Aesop was a slave and storyteller in ancient Greece. His stories are still being told 2,500 years later, which I imagine is unlikely to be true of most PowerPoint presentations we see or deliver.

It's the same with the Indian epics, the Ramayana and Mahabharata. They are great stories which enthral and have a point. The Arab world has its own storytelling traditions going back centuries, the Hakawati. The stories contained in '1,001 Arabian Nights' are part of this tradition. In Ancient Greece, rhetoric (storytelling by another name) was a key skill for anyone aiming to hold a position of influence. All these stories were passed on orally - often for centuries - before they were written down. This was only possible because they were impactful and memorable. Isn't that the aim of your presentations, too?

There is no doubt that storytelling has been to inform, teach, engage people and spur them into action for centuries. When you embrace the techniques in this book, and stand up to tell a story, rather than 'talking through slides,'. you are following the honourable traditions of Aristotle, Cicero, Aesop and in more modern times, Kennedy, King and Churchill. Or Steve Jobs in the modern business world.

Storytelling needs to be a thread that runs all the way through modern companies. The Chief Executive and other senior leaders need to be able to tell the company's story to investors, analysts, journalists and staff. Many companies organise regular Town Hall-style meetings to facilitate this. Further down the chain, managers and site heads need to be able to tell their version of the story to enthuse, motivate and inform their teams. Sales reps and other customer-facing staff rely on stories to sell their products or services. Ironically, front-line staff are often the best at telling these stories. They learn to summarise, get to the point and make it relevant to the customer because they know they have a limited amount of time. Not the only instance where the people at the top could take lessons from those ranked underneath them!

Peter Guber, Chairman and CEO of Mandalay Entertainment, says stories are like Trojan Horses. The audience accepts the story because people are wired that way. It seems like a gift. However, in reality the story is actually just a delivery system for the teller's agenda.

**A story is like a Trojan Horse -
a trick for sneaking a message into
the fortified citadel of the human mind**

Stories tap into our psyche in a way that pure data does not. In recent years, the power of the story has been backed up by science. Neuroscientists now know that our brains react differently to facts and stories. Through the use of MRI scans, they have monitored the brain activity of volunteers exposed to different types of information. When the volunteers heard facts, two parts of the brain, known as Broca's area and Wernicke's area, lit up. These parts deal with *processing information*. But when the same volunteers were told stories, up to seven parts of the brain lit up. These include the sensory cortex when they heard descriptive phrases and the motor cortex when actions were being described. These extra sections of the brain deal with *experiencing* things.

It appears that you can turn on the part of the brain that experiences something, such as a taste or a song, by describing it. A story is like a neon sign lighting up in your brain saying, 'Remember this!'

*Tell me the facts and I'll learn.
Tell me the truth and I'll believe.
But tell me a story and it will live in my heart forever.*

Native American Proverb

Neuroscientists have a phrase, 'Neurons that fire together, wire together.' This matters in storytelling because if you get it right, more regions of the brain fire in your audience, and the greater the likelihood their brains will remember what they are told. That's why, for example, medical charities tell personal stories to get you to engage and donate. They are more powerful than facts alone, and affect your brain in a different way.

The biology of the response to stories is fascinating, and the subject of an impressive body of research. It was described in the Harvard Business Review as follows::

'Oxytocin is produced when we are trusted or shown a kindness, and it motivates cooperation with others. It does this by enhancing the sense of empathy, our ability to experience others' emotions.'

These findings on the neurobiology of storytelling are relevant to business settings. For example, my experiments show that character-driven stories with emotional content result in a better understanding of the key points a speaker wishes to make and enable better recall of these points weeks later. In terms of making impact, this blows the standard PowerPoint presentation to bits.

The author of that HBR piece is Paul J. Zak, Founding Director of the Center for Neuroeconomics Studies and a Professor of economics, psychology, and management at Claremont Graduate University. You can read the article here:

https://hbr.org/2014/10/why-your-brain-loves-good-storytelling

You can do this!

One question I'm asked in my seminars is 'Can anybody learn storytelling?' The answer is yes. In fact, you're probably already doing it, but not using it in a business setting. Most of us are natural storytellers. When we are out with friends, on holiday, at work, at a big sporting event or a family party, we tell stories. Stories that make people laugh, cry, empathise, agree or sometimes disagree. Stories that engage people, and on occasion, inspire them to action. When we get home from a night out, we often retell the stories we've heard, continuing the oral storytelling tradition I outlined earlier.

Storytelling in this way is one thing that sets us apart from other animals. For thousands of years, before reading and writing skills were practised, there were only oral stories, passed down through generations. Some stories were illustrated by cave paintings; the world's first visual aids. Their precise meaning is unclear, but they included stories of hunting and other events involving animals. Once wars started, rulers and soldiers wanted something more mobile and finer than a cave wall to tell their stories, so they used elaborately illustrated tapestries. These were hung on walls, and started a process of illustration eventually leading to PowerPoint.

Storytelling is actually the subject of one of the most famous old stories – the tale of Scheherazade, a beautiful girl who saved herself from execution by the Sultan Schahriah by telling him stories for 1,001 nights. Each night she ended her story with what we would now call a cliffhanger, to be continued the following day. The Sultan couldn't bear not knowing the end of the story, so each night he spared her life until the following day, at which point she told him another story, ending with another cliffhanger. Eventually he fell in love with her, so she was spared. It's comforting to think that however much is riding on our storytelling today, our lives don't depend on it!

In Ancient Greece and Rome, storytellers were revered. The skill of capturing and retaining attention was a key attribute of educated, important men. (In those days women didn't engage in public life). Ambitious men spent many years studying rhetoric to become better storytellers and arguers.

Today, stories are an integral part of modern life. Millions of people go to the movies every year. Netflix and Amazon spend billions producing and broadcasting stories. TV series have never been so popular, and social Media is full of stories. So when we tell stories, we are doing the same thing as people have done for thousands of years. Great authors tell stories. So do documentary makers and journalists. Politicians rely on them to move people to action. Why? Because stories are special. They make points that cannot be made by facts alone.

So there's no doubt that:

- Stories are powerful, and

- We are all natural storytellers

Given this long, honourable tradition, and the fact that it works, why then do we rely on data and information-rich presentations illustrated by bulleted lists and unreadable text on a succession of dull slides?

Where is that natural storyteller when you're making a business presentation, or presenting your research findings? Where is that person when you stand behind the podium? Why is it that the moment you open a PowerPoint file you lose the power to tell stories, and resemble a corporate bot? Why is **Podium You** a monochrome imitation of **Real You**?

The answer is because too often, we stop telling stories. The next time you're near a school for little children at lunchtime, listen to the noise. It's a cacophony of kids telling stories. Shouting, screaming, but telling stories. My own daughter, now in her 20s, would burst into the house every afternoon when she came home from school shouting, 'Check this out...!! You'll never guess what's happened!!' All children are natural storytellers. Many of them become very good at it.

Something happens to our storytelling skills between the 'Check this out!' stage and the 'Next slide, please' period.

One element of the problem is that somewhere down the line, we discover PowerPoint. But I use PowerPoint, and I'm regarded as a great storyteller. It's not the fault of the PowerPoint! That's like blaming cars for road accidents. It's the driver, stupid!

In our presentations, all too often we stop telling stories that engage people and start reading slides and dumping data. We rely on slides we've used previously, or take them from a colleague. We become lazy. We present by rote, with a distinct lack of enthusiasm, or we regard the presentation as an interruption to our 'real' job. We don't dedicate enough time to preparing our talk. We just put a few slides together, and wing it. Is it any wonder that the audience are not enthused? We think it's enough to inform our audience, when in reality we also need to engage and inspire them. Informing them is necessary, but not sufficient. When people go to a restaurant they don't just want 1500 calories. They want an enjoyable, maybe even memorable experience that will add to their enjoyment. Too many presentations just deliver the calories.

All these habits are 100% understandable...and 100% wrong. By indulging them, you're killing your own chances of being a great presenter. Making presentations is a key part of your job. It's the way people spot you...so you need to be a great communicator as well as a very good doctor, IT specialist, engineer, HR person or whatever.

One of the great presenters of the 21st century was the late Steve Jobs. You may have seen clips from some of his presentations. I find them inspiring. They're models of excellence – but they didn't happen by accident. He practised, wrote, rewrote, changed the order, dropped elements when they didn't work, and practised again. He was a perfectionist, and a genius at presenting. And like all geniuses, his success was based more on perspiration than inspiration.

ABOUT THIS BOOK

The aim of the book you hold in your hands, or are reading on screen, is to encourage you to free your inner storyteller. Shake off the shackles of PowerPoint-led presentations, and put the colour back into **Podium You**. Over 25 years as a presentation coach and keynote speaker, I have watched and been involved in many thousands of presentations. I've seen a lot, learned a lot, had some great successes and made many mistakes. This book is the distillation of the key learnings. I'm going to show you how to be a good storyteller and a great presenter. I'll give you storytelling techniques and real life examples that work. I'll show you where to go to see examples of great presenters in action. I'll give you exercises which will encourage you to try out my techniques on your own material.

What do you expect from a book on storytelling? If I asked you to define storytelling, what would you say? What it does not mean is fairy stories. Anything I say about storytelling is underpinned by the idea that what you say is true and accurate. What storytelling does mean is using the information you want to convey, and turning it into a story. So when you next present, you will be impactful and memorable.

A word here about vocabulary. I use *presenting* as a term to mean *communicating verbally*. Stories are not only useful when you are presenting. There is no harm in using storytelling techniques when communicating in written form - in fact I'll do that regularly in this book. However, in this book I'm talking primarily about communicating verbally and using storytelling techniques to do that effectively. Most of them will work just as well in a written document when used *appropriately* (one of my favourite words).

A question people ask me in my storytelling seminars is, *What is the difference between a storytelling seminar and a presentation skills course?*. My answer is that I'm encouraging *storytelling,* which you can then use in a variety of situations, including presentations, interviews, videoblogs, podcasts and lectures.

However, presentation skills are only a part of my teachings, because there is more to being a great presenter than just telling stories. You need to understand how to prepare a talk, how to illustrate it, use slides appropriately, and then how to put all that together in a great delivery. This book will coach you in all of those elements.

The book is divided into three parts:

Part 1:

The three-legged stool

This looks at the fundamentals of presenting to an audience. It introduces you to the key elements of a presentation:

Content   -   Voice   -   Body Language

It also gives you some great techniques for preparing your talk quickly and simply, based on The 3 Ds:

Develop   -   Deliver   -   Defend

Part 2:

Tell stories, don't read slides!

This section goes into storytelling techniques in detail. It is packed with examples from my own 25 years' experience as a presenter and presentation coach, and prior to that, my years as a TV journalist. It includes practical techniques that you can start using, and exercises designed to let you put those techniques to work on your own presentations.

Part 3:

Are you missing the point of PowerPoint?

The problem for many presenters is that they miss the point of PowerPoint. Slides are meant to increase the likelihood of people understanding what you're telling them. Slides should be an aid to understanding and help you illustrate your story. This section shows you how to design and use slides in an engaging and clear way, producing slides that are an aid to understanding.

Examples and experience

A word about my own expertise: I work primarily in the healthcare sector. This means the people I coach are usually doctors, scientists, academics and pharmaceutical executives. I work all over the world, often with people who are presenting in their second or third language. This is a complex world, full of restrictions and regulations which can make it difficult for presenters to shine. The subject matter is often quite complicated, based on biology or chemistry. At the heart of almost every presentation, however is the question, 'So what?' or in many cases 'What does this mean to...patients, physicians, payers, the company or society?' That's a question I ask all my coachees to answer. When they can do that simply and clearly, I know we have a potentially very good presentation, however complex the subject matter.

My working life has thrown up hundreds of examples and stories. As a result, many of the examples in this book are from the scientific and medical fields. However, I would add a word of caution: Please don't be put off by the fact that so many of them are health-related. As I tend to work on complex content, the communication challenges can be huge, but the lessons I have learned from them are very relevant to you regardless of your field of expertise. If your field is also a complex one, I hope my lessons will take you from complexity to clarity. If your area is more straightforward, it may be easier to apply many of the lessons. If you work in healthcare, this book is, I hope, a treasure trove of ideas and examples.

I hope you enjoy it and find it useful.

J.C.
London
September 2018

PART 1

THE THREE-LEGGED STOOL

The key to great presentations

Picture the scene: I'm in a meeting room in a university or corporate campus, anywhere in the world. Opposite me is a senior business leader, or an internationally-known scientist. I'm here to help them develop a great presentation which will be crucial in getting their research accepted and understood, or explaining their corporate strategy to employees or investors. I've only been here a few minutes, and I've already asked them to do something unusual, perhaps something that makes them uncomfortable: Close the laptop. Disconnect the projector or screen. Put the slides away.

The man or woman sitting opposite looks at me quizzically. I adopt my best 'trust me!' expression, and explain: 'We'll get to the slides later, I promise you. But for now, I'd like you to tell me the story. Just talk to me, without slides.' I ask them to briefly tell me about the topic of their talk, whether it's their research, invention, announcement, marketing campaign or financial results.

If it's a presentation about a drug trial, I say, 'Tell me...what was the question you wanted to answer? Why is that important? How did you do the research? What did you find? What does it mean to the people in the audience?' Later, we'll get onto the objections they may face and how to handle that, but for now, let's get their story written down.

I then work with them to develop the story flow. We often start with Post-It notes. I ask them to write one point per note and then we arrange these into a narrative flow. I like this approach because the flow usually changes as we work through it, and the Post-its are easy to rearrange, discard and rewrite. When we agree the overall structure is progressing along the right lines, I transfer it to a flipchart. It's often rough, includes lots of crossings out, and is constantly amended during our session. However, it's an invaluable roadmap to their talk.

Once I've introduced the roadmap idea, we move on to what they will say, briefly summarising the main points. Finally, we get to the slides which will illustrate their talk. This is a key point. The slides *illustrate* the talk, not *lead* it. To me, writing a talk by starting with a deck of slides is, as we say in the UK, putting the cart before the horse. Putting the horse and cart in the right order would produce this sequence:

- **Ideas come first**

- **Words express ideas**

- **Slides come last.**

Preparing your presentation

When I ask scientists and medics: "How long do you spend preparing your presentation?" too often their answer is: "There's no time for that." They concentrate on the research, the data or the publication and the presentation just becomes an afterthought. The same is true in other areas of business and academia. That's the first failing.

Presentations are powerful...
and not just about the facts

Person to person communication has survived the quill, the printing press, television and the Internet. In fact, the last two have generated an enormous new appetite for good speakers.

In 1997, at Macworld in San Francisco, the world was introduced to the iPhone by Steve Jobs – a master presenter (YouTube: *Steve Jobs introduces iPhone*). Sir Ken Robinson's TED Talk has generated 40 million views. That's a remarkable audience for an academic taking about education priorities (YouTube: *Do schools kill creativity?*)

And every year, at hundreds of meetings, workshops, press conferences and the like, other highly effective orators steer scientific progress, influence their peers and advance their careers. The point here, is the enormous power of the spoken word. Getting it right requires preparation and practice.

I dread hearing the answer to my second question: "How do you start preparing your presentation?" More often than not, I hear the words *slides* and *PowerPoint*. If you only take away one lesson from this book, let it be this one.

**Effective presentations are designed
and built away from your computer.
There's lots to do before thinking about slides**

In this section I want to ask you to take a step back and think about your presentations. This is an important mental step because too often we're too busy to give any thought to our talks at all. So, I ask you now to pause, put the book or tablet down, and think about how you plan a talk. If you're honest, this is what typically happens when someone is asked to prepare a talk:

They think:

'Why me? Don't they know how busy I am?

Oh well, I suppose I'd better get on with it. It's pretty similar to a talk I gave last month/year. I'll start with those slides.

Now I'll add a few slides from a more recent talk. Wait! Didn't I see someone with a really nice slide about this? Who was it? Alice or Rohit will know...I'll email them.

Now I come to think of it, Darren had that really good slide about the forecasting versus the actual. I'll ask him for that. And I can add in that great cartoon about people falling asleep in a PowerPoint talk, and that Donald Trump Instagram photo.

[Some days later] Okay, 26 slides. 1.5 minutes per slide gives me 39 minutes. Plus five minutes for Q&A. Perfect. I'm done!'

Can you see what's wrong with this process? Firstly, it's entirely about the slides. There's no thought about the story flow or road map. The slides won't **illustrate** the talk, they will **drive** it. Secondly, this talk will inevitably be a derivative of the others, with hardly any new information, so the audience may feel short-changed. The cartoons and Trump slides may be very funny, or they may not. They may fit perfectly, or interrupt the narrative flow, with a risk that people will remember these afterwards, rather than the serious points. It also assumes there's a strict slide to time ratio (in this case 1.5 minutes). There isn't! I've seen great presentations created with only one or two slides, or even without any at all. It's the way you use them, and what you say alongside them, that matters.

I assume you've bought this book because you regularly make presentations. If so, you may even recognise some of the story outlined above. The aim of the book is to stop you thinking and behaving in that way, and to think differently. Starting from now!

Think about your next presentation. Notice the words there – it is *your* presentation. Not Alice's, Rohit's or Darren's. Yours. So make it your own. Start with these two questions:

Why am I there?

Why are they there?

Why am I there?

As this is the 21st century, there are now so many ways to communicate. Sharing information, ideas and images is quick, easy and cheap. You can use videoblogs, LinkedIn videos and articles, Facebook, Twitter, Instagram, podcasts, email, or even use your phone to dial a number and speak to another person. So why step onto the stage? In fact, why not produce the slides by the process above, and send them to anyone who's interested? Don't even bother to turn up!

In the final planning process before I'm going to speak at a conference or congress, my clients sometimes ask, 'Can you send me your presentation?'

I reply, 'No, but I could send you the slides.'

The 'presentation' consists of myself and my visual aids (which often includes slides, but also flipcharts, video and props).

If your presentation is really just your slides, ask yourself why you should bother going. Why should the audience bother going? Just send the slides and they'll get what they need. Before you plan any presentation, ask yourself, 'Why am I doing this as a presentation rather than just sending an email or letter?' The answers include:

- I can put something of myself, my own personality, into the presentation which would not be present in a published paper

- I can explain the findings in a way which is tailored to the understanding, knowledge and expectations of the audience

- I aim to be memorable, so that the audience remembers the key points

- I can answer questions and clarify misunderstandings.

Most important of all:

I am giving a talk because I have something to say, and something I want to achieve

You have a clear objective. and you saying it in your own way will mean:

- ✓ It will be memorable and clear

- ✓ People will pay attention

- ✓ Your passion and energy will be contagious, and will enthuse the audience

- ✓ You can answer questions.

All of that is true, but it is all built on the initial reason:

You have something to say

Your first step towards being a great presenter is to be clear about what that is. You need a clear objective. There are many, including:

- Making an announcement

- Sharing knowledge

- Answering a question

- Helping with understanding

- Showing you are in control
- Asking for help
- Inspiring people with a personal story

They are all, to some degree, based on altruism. There's nothing wrong with that, but preparing and delivering a talk is a lot of work, so there needs to be something in it for you, too. Such as:

- Selling something (including your ideas)
- Building your personal brand, reputation and following
- Advancing your career
- Attracting investors
- Demonstrating your wisdom, learning or other virtues
- Winning admiration and applause

Many effective presenters build an objective by picking from both lists. So, reasonable objectives might look like this:

- Sharing some new information that supports my recommended actions
- Demonstrating leadership by putting their mind at rest about rumours
- Changing attitudes, practice or behaviour
- Describing my new organisational map, to help secure my new job or role
- Lifting their spirits with amusing anecdotes, to raise my profile and ensure I an invited back

Here are some objectives from my own recent work, ie my own talks, or others which I've worked on:

- Demonstrating that, despite 20 years of failure from other companies, our new approach can herald a new era of successful research into dementia

- Convincing institutional investors that my strategy, which began two years ago, is starting to bear fruit, but we still need more time to turn the company round

- Raising money for our charity which promotes integrated education of children of all religions by showing our achievements to date

- Explaining how we are protecting our business from political turmoil in the US and the UK.

Exercise 1

Think about your next presentation. Come up with a clear, one-sentence objective for the talk and then ask yourself how you're going to achieve it. Make a few notes, which at this stage probably won't be specific enough to develop a roadmap - we will do that later.

I find a good way to help people isolate their objective is to finish this sentence:

After they have heard me, the people in the audience will...

Will what? You decide. They may:

- Be better informed

- Understand your point of view, challenges or approach

- Understand the benefits of your invention, programme or development

- Understand what you want from them and the next steps

- Think differently about your topic

- Realise there are tough times ahead, but you are planning for them

- Make a decision about my project.

Why are they there?

There are two protagonists in every presentation: You and the audience. If you ignore this simple fact, your talk will almost certainly fail. Put yourself in their shoes from the very beginning of the planning stage. Ask yourself: Why are they there? What are they expecting from me? What's in it for them? And this overlaps with the first question, 'What do I want them to do/know/think/feel or say when they have heard me?'

Preparing a presentation without an audience in mind is like addressing a love letter 'To whom it may concern'

Of all the errors committed by the presenters I work with, this is the most common one. They ignore the needs of the audience. Many of them, particularly leading academics and keynote speakers, have a regular speech, and hardly vary from it.

One internationally known speaker once said to me, 'I have a 40 minute talk. If they give me less time, I just talk faster!' I hoped he was joking, but having seen him in action, I realised he wasn't. When I was a student at journalism college in the 1970s we were told to 'write with the reader looking over your shoulder.' That piece of advice has remained with me ever since, and in recent years I've realised it's the title of a seminal book on using good English. I'm writing this paragraph with you in mind, and when I write a new talk, I have the audience in the forefront of my mind, too. In my view, you can't do it any other way. Whenever I'm asked if I'll give a talk somewhere, my first question to the organisers is 'Who's the audience?'

I have sat in many presentations, among an audience of hundreds, and wondered how many are following the speaker's words or the laser pointer. There's usually no doubt that the speaker is an expert. The problem is that he (men are more likely to commit this sin than women, in my experience) has failed to give any thought to our needs.

Here's the questions to ask yourself when you start to prepare your presentation:

Why should these people listen to me talking about this now?

What does it mean to them, and how will it change their lives/practice/understanding?

Imagine these questions are on a website. As you pass your mouse pointer over key words, hyperlinks appear. Here it is again with the hyperlinks highlighted, and points for you to consider.

Why should *these people* listen to *me talking* about this *now?* What does it *mean to them,* and how will it *change* their lives/practice/understanding?

'Why...'

The key question: What are they expecting from your talk? What do you want them to do after they've heard you? Now is a time to look again at your objective.

'...these people...'

Answer these questions about the audience. Who are they and what is their interest in your presentation? What is their level of understanding of your topic? How familiar are they with what you regard as common concepts?

'...me talking...'

What expertise and experience do you bring to the table? Are you an acknowledged authority on this topic? Do you have some unique insight? Have you conducted new research, or approached the subject differently? By <u>talking</u> to them, what will you add that couldn't be learned from an email or published article?

'...now...'

Why now? What's new or different? Have you pulled together other strands of research that had previously seemed separate? Have you filled in some missing link? How has your talk taken the subject forward?

'...mean   to   them...change   their   lives/practice/ understanding...'

The ultimate question: what's the point?   Back to your objectives: what do you want them to do after they've heard your talk? Put your research into practice immediately? Start treating patients differently? Realise that side effects can be prevented or managed by a new practice? Monitor for problems earlier? Use a new diagnostic? Understand why something is harder/easier than previously thought? Only you can decide... and you must spell it out for them.

With these questions answered, you can also consider the nature of your audience and how they prefer to receive and consider new information.

Emotional vs. intellectual

Imagine that every audience is on a scale between the two extremes of emotional and intellectual. You need to know how to appeal to them. Here's the technique:

- **To appeal to the emotions, be specific. Give them a surprising case study illustrating success or failure. Use an anecdote.**

- **To appeal to the intellect, be general. Give them the big picture, based on data. Show them the statistics.**

In reality. very few audiences are entirely emotional or intellectual...most are somewhere on the scale between the two extremes. Many will, however, veer towards one end of the other. This approach will allow you to tailor your talk as needed, or to include both techniques appropriately.

Once you know the audience, you can start gathering the information you need to make your talk relevant to them:

- How much do they know about your topic?

- How much do they need to know? How much detail do they need?

- How interested are they in it? Have they chosen or been told to attend?

- Do they all have the same level of knowledge?

- Do they know who you are? What is your relationship with them?

- What is your role? Are you being brought in as an expert in a field that is not theirs, but one they need to understand? Are you sharing your expertise as an equal, or lecturing them as an expert in their world?

- What do you want them to know/think/feel/say/do afterwards?

- What objections might they have to your argument?

- Have they had any experience of your topic – good or bad – that might influence their view of you/it?

There is much more about the audience in this book – in fact it's a major topic throughout. However, for now, I want you to consider the above questions relating to the audience when preparing for your next talk.

Exercise 2

Think about the audience for your next presentation.

Answer the questions above.

The Three-Legged Stool

There are three elements which must all combine seamlessly to produce a great presentation: Content, Voice and Body Language. I call it the three-legged stool:

I like this analogy because a three-legged stool has a number of similarities with a great presentation, both in its construction and use. Three-legged stools are flexible; their three legs allow them to be used in odd-shaped spaces (such as for milking cows) where the four-legged versions wouldn't fit. Flexibility is one of the attributes of a great presenter. All three legs have to be the same size, and all have a job do to. It's the same with content, voice and body language, or what we sometimes call verbal, vocal and visual. If any of the legs is shorter, wobbly or in some way not up to the job, the stool falls over. I'm sure you've seen it happen. It may even have happened to you. In this section, I'm going to give you some really good techniques to ensure your three-legged stool is strong, fit-for-purpose, and never lets you down.

The Mehrabian Myth

I want to address something very close to my heart: the relative weights of the three legs on the stool. In my workshops, participants occasionally mention something they've been told by other presentation coaches: That 93% of communication is non-verbal, and the content only counts for seven per cent of the meaning of a message in a presentation (or something similar). They've been told that 93% of your message is conveyed by a combination of your tone of voice (38%) and body language (a whopping 55%). This is known as the 7-38-55 rule of communication, or Mehrabian's Rule. Easy to remember, simple to quote, and backed up by references. And sadly, completely wrong in most situations.

The idea that only seven per cent of your message of conveyed by your words is complete baloney.
It's rubbish. It's not true. It's a mistake.

Just think about it: If we could understand 93% of the meaning from the non-verbals in any situation:

- How can radio and the telephone be such powerful instruments of communication?

- Why do we need to bother learning a foreign language?

- How can we communicate so effectively via online chat, text or email?

- How do an airline pilot and an air traffic controller communicate so effectively?

The seven per cent idea is nonsense in so many everyday situations: The 'No Smoking' sign in a bar, the instruction to evacuate the building when the fire alarm goes off, the STOP sign at the end of the road. All are portrayed by words alone, conveying 100% of their meaning.

If the 93% rule was accurate, should Shakespeare have written, 'Lend me your eyes?' Of course not! Yet still the Mehrabian Myth continues, propagated by mistaken, lazy or incurious presentation and communication coaches. Thankfully, many of us are the opposite of those things, and we all strive to debunk the myth. In this section I will briefly summarise Professor Mehrabian's work, what he found, and why it cannot be extrapolated to general models of communication. I'll also introduce other situations where it does have relevance.

In 1967 Albert Mehrabian, an academic at the University of California, Los Angeles, was investigating what he called the 'silent messages' in how people communicate their feelings and emotions. He limited his work in this instance to very specific circumstances: an attempt to analyse 'feelings of like-dislike' in situations where there are inconsistencies between the words spoken, the tone of voice and the body language. So he was only examining situations where:

- People were expressing feelings or attitudes, and

- They say one thing and mean another.

Here are some examples where his research does apply:

When a child asks, 'Can I stay up late on Saturday?' and the parent replies, 'Maybe'. We know the real answer is 'no', but the word doesn't tell us that. So *in those circumstances* we listen to the tone and look at the body language.

When you and your partner have had an argument. You ask them, 'Are you still angry with me?' and the other person says 'no,' although it's clear the real answer is 'yes.'

When someone seems insincere when they congratulate or commiserate with another person, 'I'm delighted to hear you're pregnant!' or 'I'm so sorry you lost your job'.

Mehrabian says that for effective and meaningful communication about emotions, these three parts of the message need to support each other - they have to be 'congruent.' If there is *incongruence*, we look beyond the words and try to find clues as to the meaning in the non-verbals.

Back in 1967 research methods were far more primitive than they are today. Mehrabian didn't actually compare the relative weight of all three elements together, but carried out two separate studies comparing words v tone of voice, and tone of voice v facial expression. All he did was to play recordings of speakers reading specific words in different tones of voice, and ask the listeners for their opinions as to the meaning. Based on these rudimentary experiments, he concluded:

Total Liking = 7% Verbal Liking + 38% Vocal Liking + 55% Facial Liking

This, in hugely simplified form, is the basis for the 7-38-55 rule, which is quoted widely, yet inaccurately.

You can read more about the details, the commentary, the criticism and the consequences by searching online for Albert Mehrabian. You can also find many communication coaches quoting the research, extrapolating the above figures to all kinds of communication and presentations.

The key mover in the campaign to 'Bust the Mehrabian Myth' is Albert Mehrabian himself. Now Emeritus Professor of Psychology at UCLA, he has given countless interviews saying, in essence, 'That's not what I said.' On his own site he says,

Inconsistent communications - The relative importance of verbal and nonverbal messages

My findings on this topic have received considerable attention in the literature and in the popular media. "Silent Messages" contains a detailed discussion of my findings on inconsistent messages of feelings and attitudes (and the relative importance of words vs. nonverbal cues) on pages 75 to 80.

And elsewhere:

Please note that this and other equations regarding relative

importance of verbal and nonverbal messages were derived from experiments dealing with communications of feelings and attitudes (i.e., like-dislike). Unless a communicator is talking about their feelings or attitudes, these equations are not applicable . Also see references 286 and 305 in Silent Messages -- these are the original sources of my findings.

Useful sources on this topic include:

The original paper, published in the Journal of Personality and Social Psychology in 1967:
http://psycnet.apa.org/record/1967-08861-001

Mehrabian's book:
Mehrabian, Albert (1981). Silent Messages: Implicit Communication of Emotions and Attitudes (2nd ed.). Belmont, CA: Wadsworth. ISBN 0-534-00910-7.

Mehrabian's website: http://www.kaaj.com/psych/

A company called Creativeworkz have produced an excellent (and very funny) video called 'Busting the Mehrabian Myth':
https://www.youtube.com/
watch?v=7dboA8cag1M&feature=player_embedded#!

However...

I don't want to dismiss the non-verbals completely. They are an important element of your presentation, but they're just not as important as some people would have you believe. The non-verbals, and indeed your voice, can act as a barrier to your content, if they are off-putting or distracting. If you've ever seen a presenter wandering around the stage without a purpose, avoiding looking at the audience, looking at their feet or out of the window, or concentrating on the screen, you'll know what I mean. However, that's a far cry from saying that the non-verbals are the dominant form of communication.

Content

Without the right content, your presentation is dead in the water. In today's corporate world, we all want the quick takeaway. That's why, in Exercise One, I asked you to summarise the objective of your talk. That's not quite the same as summarising your content. It's why I insist that my clients start with a narrative, a roadmap, before they go anywhere near their slides.

Relevance

The first point about your content is that it needs to be relevant to the audience. I'm currently writing this section on a flight to the US from London. I predict that when the Captain speaks to the passengers over the audio system as we start our approach to Philadelphia, he will say something like, 'It's a lovely day down there. With a temperature of 25 degrees and a wind speed of 15 knots from a north westerly direction, it means we'll be landing this afternoon on the south runway.' The wind speed and direction are crucially important to him (I'm delighted that he knows them!) but to me they are irrelevant. I want to know whether the flight will be on time, whether we have to get a bus to the terminal, and what flight number to look for in the baggage reclaim area.

I notice a similar tactic in many presentations. The presenter has a 'standard spiel' which they deliver, irrespective of the audience. That's why the 40 minute standard speech delivered by international thought leaders fails...it doesn't take the audience into account.

The slides are another kind of content, and we will get to that in Part 3. For now, let's focus on Part 1 of the content:

Your ideas

The French philosopher, Victor Hugo, was in no doubt about the power of ideas. He said,

There is one thing *stronger than all the* armies *in the world, and that is an* idea *whose time has* come

The problem is not that most presenters don't have enough ideas – it's that they have too many! The professor, addressing the student gathering here, sums up the problem for many experts:

"I know so much I don't know where to begin!"

Fig 1.2

Not only does he not know where to begin... he doesn't know where to stop! The problem of *knowing too much* affects many presenters. They want to show off what they know, and cover all the bases so they can't be accused of leaving anything out. This produces a talk that is over-detailed, unfocused and ultimately neither informs nor engages. If you do this, you're also failing in your duty to the audience, which is to select, prioritise, and present information in what we call the *Goldilocks Option*: 'Not too much... not too little...just the right amount of detail'.

I realise this is a difficult task, and that corralling ideas into a narrative is similar to those TV shows where cowboys try to get the wild cattle into pens. However, struggle is good for the soul, and your audience will thank you for it. So here's a foolproof technique. It starts with what we call *Media Maths*:

$$9 \times 1 = 0$$

$$3 \times 3 = 1$$

I use this when helping people prepare for media interviews, but it's equally relevant to presentations. At its most basic, it relates to the number of messages you can successfully put across in a brief interview, and how to do it. If you have nine messages and say them all once, the audience remember none. However, if you cut it down to three messages, and say them all three times, they may remember one. They may remember all three. So how do you make this relevant to your talk? Rather than three messages, you need to decide on three themes.

Medical example

Imagine you are about to present exciting new data about HIV123, a new treatment for HIV/AIDS. It really shows great promise and as far as we know, the virus doesn't become resistant to it over time, so it continues to work longer than the usual drugs, which we call 'standard of care.' HIV123 works differently from the usual treatments, and all this is achieved without the cost of any extra adverse events. Based on the data, it should be a very useful new weapon in the battle against HIV/AIDS.

Notice that paragraph above. That's the level of clarity and simplicity I encourage you to display in your own summary. You may not present it like that, but you need to be that clear about the story. In the medical world, big studies that have clear results and can change clinical practice are known as Landmark Studies. A list of them contains a brief summary of each one. The summaries are models of brevity and clarity. For example:

Finasteride in prostate cancer (NEJM, 2003)

1. Finasteride therapy was found to significantly reduce the incidence of prostate cancer compared to placebo.

2. Patients treated with finasteride were significantly more likely to have high-grade prostate cancers.

3. Patients on finasteride experienced significantly higher rates of sexual side effects including erectile dysfunction, loss of libido and gynecomastia.

The CARE trial (NEJM 1996)

1. Cholesterol-lowering therapy with statins reduces the risk of coronary events and stroke in patients with previous coronary artery disease and low-density lipoprotein levels >125 mg/dL

2. The reduction in coronary events with statin therapy was greater in women and patients with higher pre-treatment levels of cholesterol.

The JUPITER trial (NEJM, 2008)

1. Rosuvastatin significantly reduced the incidence of a first major cardiovascular event compared to placebo in healthy men and women with elevated CRP levels.

2. Rosuvastatin also significantly decreased the risk of all cause mortality by 20% compared with placebo.

You can see further examples at
www.2minutemedicine.com/the-classics-directory/

For your presentation about HIV123, your three themes might be:

- Safety

- Efficacy

- Mechanism of Action

Notice that the **themes** are not the same thing as **messages**. That's the next step. The theme is the topic. The message is what you want to say about it. So our next step is to take a piece of paper, or gather round a flipchart, and make three lists, with the messages under each theme:

Safety

Similar in both arms of trial - on drug and on placebo (dummy pill)

Adverse events were short-lived and ceased when drug stopped

Major advantage over existing drug

Efficacy

Unrivalled efficacy in hard-to-treat population

Beneficial effects seen faster than with existing drug

Non-responders identified quickly (= save money)

Mechanism of action

Different from existing drugs, based on biomarker identification

Leads to lack of resistance with current drugs

First new MoA for 20 years

These three elements will form the basis of your talk. Now you need to build them into your roadmap. I do this based on 'The Grid,' a great method of preparing your talk:

Intro	Aim	Menu 1,2,3
1:	2:	3:
Summary	Action	Close

Fig 1.3

This is how it works:

Intro and close

Start by filling in these two sections. The *intro* is your name, affiliation, and at the very least, the reason you're qualified to talk about the topic. Ideally it will also include a 'hook' to grab the audience's attention. I'll discuss different types of impactful openings in the section on delivering your talk.

The next section to fill in is the *close*. In presentations, we use it for telling the audience what will happen next, such as, 'We have a few minutes for questions now before the next speaker' or 'I'll be around for the rest of the morning and would be delighted to pick up on any of the points I've made.' Write the *intro* and *close* first. They are bookends for your talk.

Aim

Spell out a clear objective here. In the case of HIV123, you might say, 'Today I want to tell you about a new drug, HIV123, which is showing great promise in terms of efficacy, tolerability, and lack of resistance. I hope it will soon be a regular option for treatment experienced patients who've failed on earlier therapies.

Menu

Here you introduce the key themes of your talk, which you will expand on later. Limit yourself to single words or short phrases, like a newspaper headline.   Ideally you should use this as an opportunity to mention your three key messages for the first time. 'I want to divide my talk into three: It's effective, so I will show you the results of the pivotal trial....it has a different mode of action which means that resistance is unlikely to develop, and I want to show you that it's well-tolerated.

You now have the start of your talk.

Middle section

The middle section of the grid forms the bulk of your presentation. This is where you present the data, and introduce other supporting material. Notice that each of the three middle sections contains a number (1, 2 or 3) and three bullet points alongside them. The number refers to the theme for that section, and the bullets are supporting evidence. You need to introduce whatever types of supporting evidence will best support your case. For example, your three bullet points might be:

- Data

- Guidelines

- A case study

On other occasions your entire presentation might be data-focused, so your bullet points will pick out key points from a pivotal trial. This is the case on our presentation on HIV123. You might develop your plan like this:

Point 1: HIV123 is an effective ARV treatment for HIV

Bullet 1: It increases CD4+ count to above 200, the level at which we define a patient as having full-blown AIDS.

Bullet 2: It reduces viral load down to undetectable levels.

Bullet 3: Its efficacy is sustained long term, at least up to 96 weeks.

Point 2: HIV123 has a unique mode of action

Bullet 1: It works differently from other anti retrovirals, which means that resistance is rare so far.

Bullet 2: It targets the virus before it enters the host CD4 cell

Bullet 3: It stops the virus entering the cell and replicating

Point 3: HIV123 is well-tolerated

Bullet 1: In trials, the rate of adverse events on HIV123 was comparable with those on drug XYZ, the standard of care.

Bullet 2: The incidence of renal abnormalities was lower on HIV123 than on XYZ, the standard of care.

Bullet 3: A study in naïve patients showed that HIV123 had a favourable lipid profile compared with XYZ.

Summary

This is a summary of the key points, and in reality is another opportunity for you to repeat your key messages. If you think of a communication technique I outlined earlier, 'Tell them what you're going to say...Say it...Tell them what you said,' then this is the final part of that. So here you would say 'So I hope this has been a helpful introduction to this promising new treatment, HIV 123. I hope you find the efficacy data is compelling, can see how the mechanism of action produces less resistance than earlier drugs, and find the Adverse Event profile encouraging.'

Action

This is where you tell them what you want them to do as a result of having heard you. In this case, you might say, 'The question now is whether the results in practice will be as good as those in the trial. That's where you come in. I encourage you to try it...and please remember, it's for treatment experienced patients who have failed on earlier types of medication.'

Your grid might look like this:

HIV123 PRESENTATION PLAN

INTRO	OBJECTIVE	MENU
We need new anti-HIV drugs because over time, most become ineffective. Resistance is one of the biggest problems. New drugs need to be effective, tolerable and hold off resistance.	I want to show results of study on new drugs, HIV123, v drug XYZ, standard of care. They suggest it meets all our criteria and should be adapted in clinical practice.	1. Efficacy 2. Mode of Action/Resistance 3. Well-tolerated
POINT 1: EFFICACY	**POINT 2: UNIQUE MOA**	**POINT 3: WELL-TOLERATED**
Increases CD4 count above 200 Reduces viral load to undetectable levels Efficacy maintained at least up to 96 weeks	Works differently – resistance rare so far. Targets virus before tit enters hsot CD4 cell. Stops virus entering cell and replicating.	AE rate comparable to s.o.c Renal abnormalities lower than s.o.c. Study in naive patients showed favourable lipid profile compared with drug XYZ
SUMMARY	**ACTION**	**CLOSE**
Hope you agree this was a robust study v drug XYZ, which we all accept as s.o.c. HIV123 looks v promising. Lack of resistance is particularly hopeful	The question now is whether it will be as good in practice as in the trial. That's where you come in - to try it on appropriate patients who have failed earlier meds.	Now we have time for questions before we break for coffee.

Fig 1.4

Non-medical example

Imagine you're an expert in electric vehicles, and you've been invited to give a presentation to an important audience of policy makers, car sales and fleet bosses, and motoring journalists. The company sponsoring the meeting has offered test drives for many of the attendees, and the meeting looks like it will be well-attended. All you have to do is to write your keynote speech!

Using the technique outlined above, you would ask yourself (and maybe discuss with colleagues) questions such as:

- What do those people **want** to know about electric vehicles?

- What do they **need** to know?

- What do **you** want them to know?

- Are there any **myths** or **misunderstandings** you need to correct?

- What do you want them **to do** when they have heard you?

After discussions, you might come up with a presentation planning grid like this:

ELECTRIC VEHICLES PRESENTATION PLAN

INTRO	OBJECTIVE	MENU
Great day for me...been researching electric vehicles more than 20 yrs. When started, it meant milk float/golf cart!*Now...Tesla and Porsche!	Want to bring you up to date re where we are with EVs, so you understand what policies are needed, see sales opportunities and address some of the myths	1. Benefits 2. Drawbacks 3. The future
POINT 1: BENEFITS	**POINT 2: DRAWBACKS**	**POINT 3: FUTURE**
Cheaper to run Cheaper to maintain Good for the planet!!	Not enough charging points Electricity is not free Battery life 8 years average	Tesla is already worth more than Ford Big names are backing it Combing electric and driverless technology
SUMMARY	**ACTION**	**CLOSE**
Hope I've given you appetite to find out more, and not dismiss out of hand. But been realistic. 'TheFuture is electric...and driverless?'	Policymakers: Need more charge points and encouragement Fleet bosses - many benefits for you to think electric! Journalists - try them out, and stimulate debate	Now we have time for questions, then those of you who have booked a test drive can take an EV out on the track.

Fig 1.5

Exercise 3

Plan your next presentation using the 'media maths' and the grid:

Write your three key themes

Write your key three messages and three bullet points for each

Fill in The Grid

Your words and slides

I spoke earlier about the power of ideas. Now let me give you another thought:

**Ideas stand or fall based on
how they are conveyed**

Your great ideas are worthless if, conceptually, if not commercially, you're unable to sell them. All presenters are salespeople now. It's not just your idea you're selling. There's also yourself, your company or department, institution or faculty, your vision, your product, your energy, your team and many other elements. The overall success of all this is based on how well you convey the ideas, and that means using the right words.

**Prose - words in their best order
Poetry - the best words in the best order**

Samuel Taylor Coleridge

Let's leave the poetry to the poets, or at least until Part 2 of this book, on storytelling. For now, you have your ideas, mapped out into a narrative structure. The next step is to work out how you're going to express them, verbally and on screen (assuming you will be using slides). In your presentation, the words coming out of your mouth need to have a clear relationship with the slides. They should work in tandem to make your arguments clear for the audience. It is vital, therefore, that you plan for this, and make sure the one complements the other.

There are a number of ways to achieve this. Personally, I work out the first draft of the words, then design the slides to support them. This process usually creates other ideas for the words, which in turn feeds into the slides I need, so I go back and forth between the words and slides. This is a very good process, because when I come to make the presentation, I'll be doing the same thing, constantly moving between my words and the information on the slides.

I find that many presenters don't think too much about the words they're going to say. They concentrate on the narrative flow and the slides. This is a mistake. Words are powerful. As the brilliant UK Telegraph newspaper campaign says, *'Words are powerful. Choose them well.'* The video is a great illustration of the power of words. https://www.youtube.com/watch?v=cuUolL-kOy8

Look at the difference in power between 'thought,' 'vision' and 'dream,' or 'dodge,' 'weave' and 'float' or 'misleading,' 'inaccurate' and 'fake,' and you will see the power of the English language. Read some of the great speeches from Martin Luther King, Winston Churchill or JFK, and see how they use language. These words are not used by accident. The authors have thought deeply about them, discussed them, tried and rejected alternatives, and finally decided on just the right combination. The problem is that so many presenters pay little or no attention to their words. They decide to 'talk through the slides' and say, 'I don't have time to prepare the words...they just come out of the slides.' Others say they use the slides as a prompt for what to say next. All of these statements, whilst understandable, are steps on the way to misusing PowerPoint. Here's an initial thought:

Don't use your slides as a teleprompter

If the words on the slides are just the same as the words coming out of your mouth, we don't need them both

If you only read the slides, you're writing yourself out of the script. You need to add to what's on the screen. You can do this in many ways: Add context or explanation, express surprise or pleasure. Tell us what's important and where to look. Use conversational language. Talk as you would normally speak when telling a story. Go back to the narrative flow you developed at the start when I said, 'Tell me about your research, your talk, your product.' What words did you use then? Use the same words now.

Interacting with your slides

A great presentation is a coming together of the presenter, the visual aids and the audience. In this final section I want to give some tips for the way you interact with your visual aids. In the majority of cases, this will mean PowerPoint slides, so I'll concentrate on using them.

Use signposts

The 'signposting' technique tells the audience where you're taking them next on this journey. It often closes one section and opens another. It's a really important element of interacting with your slides. You might say, 'So that's the data on the drug's effect on the liver. There's been some concern expressed about potential effects on bone formation, and that's where I'd like to turn now.' Then, and only then, do you reveal the next slide, on bone markers. It's important to do it in this order, because for those few important seconds the audience will concentrate on what you're saying. If you reveal the slide and then say it, they'll be trying to figure out what's on the slide, and may miss what you say.

Pause and introduce the slide

Although you're very familiar with your slides, each one comes as a surprise to your audience. Once you reveal a new slide, the first thing you must do is pause and explain the layout. This is particularly important in the early part of the presentation, when you're familiarising your audience with the appearance of the slides as well as their content. You need to explain the axes, the scales and the colours. You might say, 'The vertical axis is the drug concentration, the horizontal one is time (in hours) since the last dose. The blue curve is the control group, and the yellow one is the treatment group.

Tell them what's important

Given the subject matter, and however much we try to simplify it, some slides still end up looking quite complicated. Here, building up a slide can help, and I will outline this in Part 3 of the book. Even then, you need to tell the audience what's important. When presenting Kaplan-Meier survival curves, you might say, 'If you look here, you'll see that the curves separate quite quickly, and by the end of the study there was an overall survival difference of 5.4 months. This is why the trial was stopped early. The Ethics Committee decided it was unethical to keep patients on the placebo group, when those on the treatment arm were gaining such a significant benefit.'

If you're presenting the design of a number of trials, you might say, 'What is important here is this figure: the percentage of patients who continued from one study to the next...93%. That's a great vote of confidence from the patients, as it's a measure of their benefit and satisfaction with the experimental therapy. One would hope, though obviously we can't prove this yet, that it may lead to improved adherence in clinical practice.'

One difficulty for an audience who are unfamiliar with the details is the ability to understand whether a big or a small number is beneficial, or whether a reading should go up or down. Sometimes a trial includes values you want to increase, and others you want to reduce. Simple examples are that you generally want to reduce blood pressure and LDL cholesterol, but increase HDL cholesterol and T-scores on a bone mineral density test. You want to normalise blood glucose and INR levels. It can be disconcerting to an audience, when, if all the previous slides have contained values that have gone up from baseline, you suddenly present a slide where they all go down. There's a simple solution to this...tell them! Make it clear what you're aiming to do, and what success would look like when measured on this parameter.

Voice

Some years ago I went on a public speaking course taught by actors at RADA, the *Royal Academy of Dramatic Art* in London. One of the exercises we were asked to undertake has stuck in my mind. We were each given a number from 1 to 10, unseen by the others. We were all to sit around a table, as if in a meeting, and the chosen one had to come in and say 'Excuse me.' Just that. Two words. We had to say these words based on the number we'd been given. So whoever was given number 1 had to be quiet, shy, embarrassed and reluctant to interrupt, while the person with 10 had to play a bombastic, boorish, over-confident and loud individual. Once we had made our entrance, the other students had to try and guess our number.

The point of the exercise was to introduce us to one of the most important techniques in public speaking: Vocal Variety. It was a simple exercise, but hugely successful in quickly showing us what an amazing asset we have in the human voice. It introduced us to the world of the vocal toolbox so effectively that now, 20 years later, I still remember it.

Since then I've come to appreciate the extent to which the human voice is our most powerful instrument, and how it is infinitely adaptable. The voice is the only instrument played by every one of us. However, as the composer, Richard Strauss, said,

The human voice is the most beautiful instrument of all, but it is the most difficult to play

Yet, when someone has mastered it, what an impact they have on the rest of us! As the Irish opera singer Anna Devin said,

There's a human instinct within us
that connects us through our voice

Just consider, for a moment, the skill and technique of an opera singer. Their voice needs sufficient power to fill an opera house, to carry without amplification and be heard clearly above an orchestra of up to 100 musicians. And they're not shouting... they're controlling their breathing, hitting and holding the notes, and doing it with such power and emotion they can reduce us to tears. Think of a baby crying ...the cry is impossible to ignore, and research suggests it lights up areas of the brain not affected by any other sound. https://www.theguardian. com/science/2012/oct/17/crying-babies-hard-ignore

Whether it's used for speech or song, the human voice has the power to move millions. Listen to any of the great opera singers, or tune in to the annual 'Carols from King's' Christmas service on the BBC, opened by the young male soloist singing 'Once in Royal David's City'. Listen to an acapella song, or Freddie Mercury at Live Aid, or Lennon and McCartney, or whatever suits your musical taste. In our personal lives we use it all the time. We sing for love, sorrow or joy. We sing and chant at sports stadiums, and in church. In the UK, two million people a week sing in amateur choirs, and the FA Cup Final crowd singing 'Abide With Me' still stirs the hearts of many, football fans or not.

When used for the spoken word, the voice can bring sorrow and joy. It can declare war and say 'I love you.' Throughout history, human voices have been used to provoke change, spur millions into action, or calm mutinies. It has moved people to heights of achievement, or the depths of tragedy. The Ancient

Greeks and Romans regarded oratory as a key attribute for anyone seeking public office. We can change the tone so it can be commanding, pleading or declaring. A change in volume can take us from shouting to whispering, depending on our emotional state and, the context or the dramatic effect we seek.

The human voice: it's the instrument we all play. Why is it, then, that when we take to the stage, we underuse it to such a degree? It's as though we go on stage with a Stradivarius violin, a Steinway piano or a Fender guitar, and then ignore it. There's a Chinese proverb which says :

The tongue can paint what the eye can't see.

I talk more about this in Part 2 of the book, about storytelling. For now, it's worth noting that part of your job as the presenter is to 'paint what the eye can't see', ie add to the details on the slides, as outlined in the 'content' section above. Sadly, many presenters don't do this properly, because they don't pay attention to their voice. In fact, the 'voice' leg is the most neglected in the three- legged stool.

This is a mistake in any presentation, but there is one circumstance when the misuse of your voice can be the kiss of death: when you're presenting by teleconference or telephone. This strips away all your other communication tools and leaves you with just one: your voice. It's difficult enough to gain and keep people's attention when you're not physically present, but to then present in a bored monotone, as many people do, is a guaranteed way to lose them.

When I run classes on how to present via teleconference, I ask participants to leave the room and present to us from another room, so we can't see them. I record their voice from the phone and when they return to the room, I play it back to them. I've done this many times, and I've never met anyone who is not at least surprised, and often horrified by how flat, unengaged and frankly dull they sound. You should try it!

To illustrate the opposite end of the spectrum, and see vocal power in action, check out The Jersey Boys' movie where the young Frankie Valli sings, 'Sherry' down the phone line to the record company boss, and wins a recording contract. Recently I found a similar example when listening to a radio interview with American folksinger Peggy Seeger. She was once married to the singer/songwriter, Ewan McColl. During the interview she told the story that one day she rang him and said she needed 'A love song that was under two minutes'. He said he'd been working on something based on the first time he saw her, and sang it to her down the phone. It was 'The First Time Ever I Saw Your Face', which became a global hit. You may not have the vocal skills of Franki Valli, or the songwriting talent of Ewan McColl, but you do have a voice. I hope these stories inspire you to think more about how you use it!

Seven Deadly Sins you can Commit with your Voice (and how to fix them)

1. Never listening to yourself giving a talk

If you have ever played golf or tennis, and had video coaching, you know how painful it can be. Most people feel the same about their voice. Most people hate hearing themselves, but if you don't put yourself through that ordeal, how do you know what you sound like?

How to fix it

Next time you give a talk, ask someone to record it for you. Or just set your smart phone to video, and press record as you start to speak. Don't worry about the video at this stage. In fact, don't look at the video, but concentrate on the sound of your voice. Speak clearly, in your 'presentation voice.' Now play it back. If you're really self-conscious about it, take the recording somewhere private...the bathroom, your car, or the top of a mountain. Recording yourself and listening to it back is the single thing you can do to improve your vocal presentation skills.

2. Speaking in a monotone

This is one of the world's great mysteries to me: Why do people who speak perfectly normally in everyday conversation become monotonous once they're on stage? It gives a terrible impression and means that they're missing a key reason for giving the talk... so that their voice can help the audience to understand. You need vocal inflection, the rising and falling of pitch and tone, to add energy and variety to what you say. When used properly, your voice can be a valuable pointer to the audience, helping them to identify the key points in your talk.

Sometimes presenters sound bored because they are. They've seen the slides before, they've given the talk 50 times, and they're bored with it. Don't be. It may be the 50th time for you, but it's the first for the audience. Some presenters, especially in the scientific and academic worlds, believe their data can speak for them, and become the dull soundtrack to the slides. Don't do this!

How to fix it

To avoid this, try recording yourself telling a personal story, and listen to the modulation, the rise and fall, the variety. Then record yourself giving a talk, and aim for the same amount of vocal variety and energy.

3. Reading the slides

If all you're going to do is read the slides, just send the slides! If you do this, you're writing yourself out of the script! In addition, if you read the slides, the audience will do that too, and get to the end of each one faster than you can, because they're reading silently. This sometimes encourages some presenters to go faster.

How to fix it

Design your slides so that you have something to add. You should always add to what's on the slide. You can add context, explanation, justification, or comment. You can tell us your reaction to the results. Don't put it all on the slide. Avoid too much text, as that will encourage you to read it.

4. Speaking too fast

There are a number of reasons for this: The adrenalin rush, a fear that we have too much material for the time slot, a worry that the audience isn't really interested, or a strong desire to 'Get it over with as quickly as possible.' Whatever the reason, speaking too fast detracts from the power of your words.

How to fix it

The problem begins when we're first briefed about our talk. The organisers say. 'You have a 20 minute slot.' How many words is that? As a guide, TV and radio presenters working in English speak at about three words a second, or 180 words a minute. Type out 360 words on your favourite topic, written to be read aloud, then record yourself doing just that. Read them as though you were presenting them to an audience, with energy and intonation. That should take you about two minutes. If not, adjust your speed. Once you've got it right, that's your benchmark.

5. No pauses

The power of the pause is a wonderful thing. We use it for a number of reasons: to let the audience understand the implications of what we've said or for effect; to separate items in a list; to slow down the overall speed of our talk. Presentations without pauses risk becoming vocally monotonous. We also use it for dramatic effect. If I'm presenting and I say, 'This is the most...' and then I pause, the audience are hanging on what comes next. It's a moment of drama.

How to fix it

Work out in advance where you can build in pauses to the greatest effect and then practice it. If you have a written script, or cue cards, write 'PAUSE HERE!' on them in the appropriate place.

6. Talking to the screen

This is among the most common mistakes made by presenters, and one I'll discuss further in the section on body language. For now, bear in mind that if you don't look at the audience, your voice will be projected away from them. In addition, if the microphone is fixed to the podium, it will not pick up your voice when you look away from it.

How to fix it

A tendency to screen-read is often exacerbated by very busy slides, which demand to be read line by line. Keep text on slides to a minimum. When you're presenting, ensure your feet are pointing at the audience, not at the screen. Record yourself on video, and notice the extent of the problem. You need a relationship with the screen and the audience, but your attention should be primarily on them rather than the screen.

7. We can't hear you!

However brilliant your words, if we can't hear them, they're wasted. Much of the time you'll have a microphone, so this shouldn't be a problem. However, even this is no guarantee. Just last week the batteries in my lapel microphone failed on me. The AV man quickly gave me a hand-held mic, and that didn't work either. So I stood behind the podium, which had a fixed mic, and it was fine. It wasn't perfect as, when appropriate, I like to walk around the room. However, given that I was talking about presentation skills, I turned it into a lesson. I said to the audience, 'Okay...so now two mics have failed. What would you do?'

How to fix it

Ask about the set-up in advance. On the day, get there early, and check the AV set up. Check you know how to use that particular microphone – how close to hold it to your mouth, whether you speak across it or into it, and the volume it produces. In short, practice with it before you're on. And be clear about where you can stand to avoid amplifier/speaker feedback!

Body Language

We use video cameras in my presentation workshops to record and critique the participants' presentations. Once a participant has presented to the group, my routine is always the same. I say, 'Thank you for your talk. Now I have a question to the group. What do we think of X?'

Bearing in mind I mainly work with scientists and senior executives who are a pretty intellectual bunch, it's still surprising that most of their answers start with the body language. They say things like, 'He didn't look comfortable...' 'She looked defensive when she talked about....' 'He looked quite cold...' 'His body language was arrogant...' Note that I do NOT ask about the body language specifically, but it regularly comes up as the first thing people mention. This shows us the impact it can have in our professional lives, particularly in presentations.

Body language, surprisingly, is a two-way street: It affects the way others see us, and may even have an impact on the way we see ourselves. Our body language sensors are always active, but they are turned up to maximum sensitivity when we are watching a presentation. Even subconsciously, decisions we make about presenters are based partly on how they use and move their body. Without body language, silent movies would never have taken off. In the modern TV era, Mr Bean is one of British TV's most successful exports, enjoyed by millions of people who don't speak English. Watch how stand-up comedians use and move their body for maximum effect. Or watch a great TED talk with the sound turned off.

Many of us love people watching, usually when we're in a busy place such as a coffee shop, a bar, an airport or a hotel lobby. Sometimes we make assumptions, even invent stories about the people we're watching, based on their body language.

I'm a photographer and I enjoy street photography. I approach strangers in the street and ask if I can take their picture. They rarely refuse, partly because I've pre-selected those I think will be amenable to it, based on their body language (as well as being visually interesting!).

There is even evidence that suggests body language doesn't just affect how people see you, it can also affect how you see yourself. Harvard Psychology Professor Amy Cuddy's research says that by adopting what she called 'high power poses' for just two minutes, you can raise your testosterone (the dominant power hormone) and reduce your cortisol (the stress hormone). Her technique has been described as, 'Fake it till you make it,' but she says it should be, 'Fake it till you become it.' Her TED talk is compelling, and an excellent example of how to give a great presentation: https://www.ted.com/talks/amy_cuddy_your_body_language_shapes_who_you_are#t-3640

She also shows that the candidates who are most likely to be hired in job interviews exhibited these characteristics:

- Confidence

- Passion

- Enthusiasm

- Authenticity

- Comfort

- Captivation

Taken together, these add up to that elusive, and difficult-to-define quality of 'presence.' They are the same body language characteristics which signal a great presenter.

Body Language: Essentials

Here are the key elements of body language in a presentation:

Authority

Nobody enjoys watching a nervous presenter. The first thing your audience want to feel is that you're comfortable in this situation. This requires feeling confident in a number of aspects: Your subject overall, the material you're going to present, and the reaction you anticipate from your audience. The question is: how do you demonstrate authority?

An audience will make up their mind about you within a very short time, so make sure you start correctly. Remember that first impressions last, and that you only get one chance to make one. Slow down, be measured, wait until the Chair has finished introducing you and then walk briskly onto the stage. The timing is important. It's quite common to be sitting in the front row while you're being introduced. If this is the case, don't upstage the Chair by walking up while he/she is talking. Depending on the setting, I sometimes stand to the side of the stage, ready to walk on when they've finished speaking. I aim to make my stance look confident and authoritative, without upstaging the Chair. I listen to what he/she is saying, and I never, ever look at my notes at this stage. If I need to look at them now, I don't know my topic! It's also rude to ignore what the Chair is saying about me, so I usually look at him/her, or at the audience.

I walk on stage, shake their hand if appropriate, thank them for their introduction, and pause for a few seconds, from behind the lectern if there is one, or if not, from the middle of the stage. Smiling is important here. It suggests you are looking forward to what's coming, welcomes the audience, shows you are human and relaxes your facial muscles. Try and make a reference to what the Chair has just said about you. If appropriate (that word again!), make a little joke. If I've been introduced in a particularly effusive way, I sometimes say, 'Thank you...that's very kind. And after that introduction, I'm looking forward to hearing what I have to say.'

Using the other techniques outlined in this chapter will also create a feeling of authority.

Energy

The seventh sin in my book 'The Seven Deadly Sins of Scientific Presentations (and how to avoid them)' is 'No performance in your presentation.' You need to ask yourself, 'Why am I giving this as a talk, rather than just sending the slides?' One reason is that you can be more impactful and memorable as a presenter. To do this you need to be energetic.

I've given similar talks many times, yet people often compliment me on my energy and obvious enjoyment of the subject matter. I take this as a huge compliment. Once again, I find similarities with actors who go on stage to perform the same play night after night. If I go to see the 200th (or 500th!) performance of a show, I want it to be as lively and energetic as the first night. After all, it may be the 200th time for the actors, but it's the first time I've seen it. Your presentations should be the same...so you need to show energy. Think of the powerful presenters you know, and consider what sets them apart. One major factor is the energy they put into the performance. From the moment they bound onto the stage you can sense their physical energy, which acts like a lightning conductor to the audience...it energises them all and makes them sit up in anticipation. Isn't that how you want your audience to react?

Passion

Passion in an overused word today. On TV, radio and online, politicians claim they are passionate about social mobility, education, reducing greenhouse gases, cutting taxes or whatever subject is on today's agenda. No doubt, some of them are. However, this is not the kind of passion you need in a presentation. In this sense, passion means showing that you are enthralled by, and engrossed in, not only in your subject, but also the opportunity to tell other people about it. I think of it as enthusiasm + emotion. It's easy to recognise, and impossible to fake. It comes from a combination of all three legs of the stool...your body language, voice and content, and it's true that some subjects are easier to get passionate about than others for some people. I will address this in Part 2 of the book, and show you how creating 'memorable moments' can create passion. If you need motivation, think about the subject 'Global health trends 1962 – 1997.' You may think that's a pretty dry subject. However, in the hands of Professor Hans Rosling, it's a riveting masterclass: https://www.ted.com/talks/hans_rosling_shows_the_best_stats_you_ve_ever_seen#t-126784

Gestures
There are two types of gestures that matter:

- What do you do with your body?

- What do you do with your face?

Your body

Bodily gestures, in particular, need to be *appropriate* and *inclusive*. The first rule is to use your hands. Don't stand there like an unwilling participant in a police line-up. It's notable how many presenters say to me, 'I don't know what to do with my hands.' Well, what do you normally do with them? Mostly, you use them for gesture, emphasis or phrasing and sometimes for ticking off items on an imaginary list. Do that on stage. However, your 'usual' gestures that you use in everyday conversation are normally too constrained, to small and low, to work on a big stage. On stage you need to be bigger, more expressive, more energetic. So make your gestures slightly grander, and raise your hands higher.

Good stage gestures come from the shoulders, not from the wrists or elbows.

As a presenter, you need to grow and shrink your gestures to make them match the room. Grand gestures don't necessarily work if you're in a small meeting room, presenting to a handful of people. That's where the concept of *appropriate* gestures comes in. On stage in front of 500 people you need to own the space. You can pace around, as long as you do it with purpose. Vary your gestures, and stand still for some of it. Then when you stride to the edge of the stage to address a certain section of the crowd for one part of your talk, then to the left for the next topic, your movements will appear dramatic and have purpose. Just as when you use your voice you need to understand the power of *silence*, when you move your body you need to understand the power of *stillness*. Your gestures can be expansive, with wide, sweeping arm movements as you demonstrate confidence and authority. In front of half a dozen colleagues in an informal review meeting you would generally be advised to tone things down, and settle for more limited gestures. We've all been in meetings where someone who doesn't understand the form goes 'over the top,' which ultimately doesn't do anything for their credibility. The converse is also true...if you don't display an animated personality on the big stage, it can swallow you up and you'll find yourself less than memorable.

An *inclusive* gesture is one which includes the audience, such as opening your arms out wide with palms facing outwards. An *exclusive* gesture is one which excludes all or part of the audience. Turning your back on the audience to point at the screen with a laser pointer is an exclusive gesture. It might also mean that they can't hear you, as you go 'off-mic'.

I know that some presentation coaches advise against using laser pointers. I believe this is wrong. Laser pointers do have a place in the presentation of complicated data or images, (eg medical and scientific data) when used appropriately. This means pointing out key parts of a table, curves or forest plots, for example. They are indispensable when showing images of tumours, X rays, angiograms and similar diagnostic tools. The secret is to use the laser where needed, and to point clearly at the target. Avoid the 'laser whirls' we see so often, where the presenter feels they need to use the laser on every slide. You don't need it on most slides.

Variety is another important element of gesturing. Vary the moves you make. To check this, record yourself on video and play it back on fast-forward. This will reveal your body language in exaggerated fashion, and you'll then be able to modify it accordingly.

It isn't only your own gestures that are important. When I make a presentation I'm also constantly looking at the audience, judging how my talk is being received. I'm also watching for gestures of agreement from them. Usually, this is a slight nod. When people nod it suggests agreement, and gives me confidence that they have understood my point. I then work to make them nod again to my next point, and so on.

Your face

(especially your eyes)

Your face is your key instrument when making a connection with the audience. They need to see your face, and wherever possible, you need to see theirs. That's one reason why talking to a camera at an external location is so difficult ...we look for facial clues in our listeners and audiences.

Facial gestures are what makes us human. That's why we smile when we see other primates using them. The first thing you should do with your face is smile. And smile properly, not in some rictus grin (even if you're nervous). Smiling, crucially, involves the eyes, and they are *so* important. 'There are many expressions relating to the importance of eye contact: 'The eyes are windows on the soul,' 'I want to see the whites of their eyes.' 'Look me in the eye and tell me this won't go wrong.' 'He looked shifty, and refused to look me in the eye'. All these apply when you're making a presentation. (Unlike the claim that it takes twice as many muscles to frown as it does to smile. Check it out.)

After smiling with your eyes, use them to look at the audience. It's important to look around at everyone, so they all feel included. Let them see your eyes. Then they can see if you're excited, sad, happy, bored, distracted or focused. Some presenters think that on stage in front of a big audience, their eyes can't be seen. This is no longer true because many auditoriums now have video cameras built in, so your face is being shown on a big screen.

When I go on stage I always try to include the extremities of the audience in my eye contact. I look at the ends of the front row, left and right, and at the ends of the back rows. I usually find a small number of people in the audience to focus on, to build a rapport with as representatives of the audience as a whole. I encourage them to nod, smile or interact with me in any other appropriate ways.

During the talk, your face provides crucial cues to the audience to back up your words and tell them what you expect them to do or feel. You can smile, frown, look surprised, mock-shocked, worried, serious or elated. Whatever you do, just as with your body language, in front of a big audience you need to exaggerate the expression.

Actors learn how to use not only their overall body language, but also their faces, including micro-expressions. These are instant expressions lasting a fraction of a second which are used to convey emotions, including disgust, anger, fear, sadness, happiness, surprise and contempt. Some psychologists claim they offer a clue to our true feelings. Whether that's true or not, our human instinct can pick up on them immediately, so we need to know when and how to use them as part of our communication repertoire.

Look at the audience

The most common body language issue with the people who attend my courses is the amount of time they spend looking at the screen, rather than at the audience. It comes as a surprise to many of them too. There are many reasons for this, but the main one is that their slides are too busy, text-based and need reading. I discuss this in detail in Part 3. For now, concentrate on looking at the audience rather than the screen. Refer to the points I made earlier about your voice, including checking where your feet are pointing.

However, it's important to realise here that not all presentations are the same. Sometimes you're showing slides containing data, information or ideas that you want to *discuss* rather than *present*. This is quite common at medical or scientific meetings, and usually happens in a small group of colleagues, fellow scientists or other peers. It's very common in slide review meetings, where the presenters go through their proposed presentations with others involved. In these situations it's perfectly accept- able, even expected, to turn to the screen and talk, picking on specific data points to discuss.

However, it is not acceptable to do this in your main pre- sentation. Here, you need to refer to the information on the slide, and ensure the audience knows what you're trying to tell them. However, for most of it, you should face them and not the screen.

Female challenges

I've had the privilege of working with some great presenters, both male and female. I mention this because women sometimes ask me whether I see any difference between the sexes in terms of presentation skills. My short answer is 'no,' at least not in the sense that women need to present differently. My view is that everyone needs to develop their own personal presentation style, and this should be based on their own attributes. This is based on personality and style, not gender.

Everything I've talked about so far applies equally to men and women. You need to be authentic, the best version of yourself, appear confident and talk in a way that is both relevant to the audience and the setting. However, in some settings there are some traits that work better with men than women, or vice versa, as Hillary Clinton observed:

"If you want to run for the Senate, or run for the Presidency, most of your role models are going to be men. And what works for them won't work for you"

**'Women are seen through a different lens.
It's not bad. It's just a fact.'**

"It's really quite funny. I'll go to these events and there will be men speaking before me, and they'll be pounding the message, and screaming about how we need to win the election. And people will love it. And I want to do the same thing. Because I care about this stuff. But I've learned that I can't be quite so passionate in my presentation. I love to wave my arms, but apparently that's a little bit scary to people. And I can't yell too much. It comes across as 'too loud' or 'too shrill' or 'too this' or 'too that.' Which is funny, because I'm always convinced that the people in the front row are loving it."

Most of us, however, are unlikely to find ourselves on the campaign trail. In more common business contexts, I find little difference.

BBC TV News presenter Maxine Mawhinney coaches female leaders all over the world on their presentation skills. She said,

The Hillary experience is interesting in the fact that she felt she couldn't get her message across in the same way as the men. Some of that will have been down to the marmite effect of Hillary but her experience is not hers alone. Women I work with often say they cannot use the same body language or speak at the same volume as their male counterparts usually for the same reasons as Hillary has given. But that does not mean they are any less effective – it comes down to finding their own personal style delivered with a confidence that demands attention.

In particular, they need:

- *Strong body language without aggressive movement;*

- *Modulated voice – a woman's voice can become higher in certain situations*

- *Incisive and positive interrupting when appropriate*

- *To resist exclusion in an all-male room*

In one-to-one coaching, high-flying female executives will usually reveal their weaknesses and vulnerability more readily than men, and have a determination to work to improve themselves. They look for female role models. Fortunately today there are many.

Former US Secretary of State (and first woman in the job) Madeleine Allbright said she would sit at a table with men and not make her point, not interrupt and then her moment was gone. Or hold back on a comment only for a man to make it and be praised. Her advice is 'Don't hold back.'

'I have said this many times, that there seems to be enough room in the world for mediocre men, but not for mediocre women, and we really have to work very, very hard.'

My advice to women (and men) is don't copy others as you will lose yourself and your authenticity. Instead look for things that you can take and make your own.

The Seven Deadly Sins

To close this section, here are *The 7 Deadly Sins of Scientific Presentations*, from my e-book of the same name. And remember, they don't only apply to *scientific* presentations!

Sin #1: Too much information

Sin #2: Ignoring the needs of the audience

Sin #3: Dense, unclear or confusing slides.

Sin #4: Letting your slides run the show

Sin #5: No performance in your presentation

Sin #6: No attention-grabbing opening

Sin #7: Weak endings

Part 1 - Summary

You need to *own* the presentation.

Ideas come first
Words express ideas
Slides come last

When planning your talk, ask yourself:

- Why am I here?

- Why are they here?

The three-legged stool is the key to great presentations:

Content - Voice - Body Language

To clarify your thoughts, summarise your talk in a sentence or two.

Use the grid to plan your presentation

Tailor your talk to fit your audience

Don't use your slides as a teleprompter

Your voice is a powerful and underused instrument

Your body language should project authority, energy and passion

Talk to the people, not the screen

Be aware of the two main types of gestures:

- Facial

- Bodily

PART 2

"TELL ME A STORY"

Shakespeare was a playwright with a problem. His dramas were performed in rowdy theatres full of noisy, boisterous drinkers, who whilst having a great time, enjoyed heckling and booing if they didn't like what was happening on stage. That's a tough crowd. Shakespeare had two major challenges:

- **How to grab their attention**
- **How to keep their attention**

These are two of the most common questions I hear in my storytelling masterclasses. Shakespeare addressed the first challenge by coming up with strong dramatic openers. *Macbeth* opens with th witches on a stormy heath, Hamlet with scared castle guards and talk of ghosts. He addresses the second by having strong characters and by keeping the story moving with plot twists, intrigue and drama. Most importantly, he tells a good story. He also produces a presenting masterclass in *Julius Caesar,* where Anthony gives his speech at Caesar's funeral. Here, Anthony has a clear objective – to rouse the crowd against Caesar's killers. He uses a prop (Caesar's body) and theatrical pauses ('Bear with me, my heart is in the coffin there'). His key message, 'Brutus is an honourable man' is repeated 10 times to ensure the audience grasp the sarcasm. These are all classic storytelling techniques, which I'll examine in detail in this section.

Shakespeare's problems are your problems, updated for the modern age. Imagine we're at a conference, or another important meeting. A new speaker takes the stage. How long before we decide this is going to be interesting? Psychological research provides answers ranging from a fraction of a second to half a minute. Those estimates apply, however, to job interviews and blind dates too. Surely that's not relevant to our world of serious presentations? Well, yes and no.

Of course, a speaker at a scientific meeting gets longer than a few seconds to make a favourable impression, but the concept remains valid.

You only get one chance to make a first impression...
so make sure it's a good one

Great openings

The British athlete, Linford Christie, won the 100 metre gold medal at the Barcelona Olympics. He dedicated the medal to his coach, with the words, 'He got me to go from the B of the Bang.' Going from the 'B of the Bang' of the starting gun is clearly crucial for Olympic sprinters, but what's the equivalent for presenters? Later in this book, we'll consider body language and voice control and how these can help to make a strong impression. But here, let's focus on what you say. You need to start with an attention grabber. When I work with presenters, I urge them to think very hard about their opening. You should do the same.

I have a number of potential openings to suit different audiences, and I'm always inventing new ones. I often start by asking questions about what they like and dislike about presenting, getting the audience to raise their hands in response. This has the added benefit of giving me an indication of their own presenting experience.

Sometimes I start with a photograph of Albert Einstein, and a quote attributed to the great scientist: *"Everything should be made as simple as possible, but no simpler."* This is very good advice for scientific presenters and their accompanying slides. How do you judge 'as simple as possible, but not too simple?' The best answer depends on many things ... the complexity of the subject, the knowledge and interest of the audience, the length of your talk. It's up to you. In the next half-hour, I'll help you decide ...so you can deliver talks that really resonate with your audiences.

Sometimes I start with a photograph of my father and I and say *'I'd like you to meet my Dad. Like many people of his generation, he took up smoking when he was about 14. He was still smoking in his 60s, despite my years of nagging at him to stop. He thought it was too late, the damage had been done. Then one day I interviewed a professor about the health benefits of quitting at any age and showed the interview to my Dad. After more than 50 years, my Dad stopped smoking."* This leads me to my first key point: 'Information is not communication.'

Given my role as a presentation coach, I make a lot of presentations. This gives me the opportunity to try things out and judge the audience's reaction. I do this all the time, to ensure my talks remain fresh. So don't just come up with one opener and stick with it. Develop a number of openers for different situations.

I've seen a lot of excellent attention-grabbing openers...and some very bad ones. Generally, the bad ones failed because they didn't engage the audience, or worse, they drove home an insult.

I saw a big name American professor confuse and irritate an audience of European physicians with this opening remark: *"Okay...who supports the Colts here? No Colts? Okay, who's going for the Bears? What, nobody here from Chicago? Well that's a surprise."*

Really? The disappointing surprise here was the presenter. He failed to understand his audience. A little research would have told him the Super Bowl and American Football have a tiny following in Europe. Were there likely to be any fans of the Chicago Bears or the Indianapolis Colts in that room? Worse, most of his audience spoke English as a second language, so few understood: *"Who's going for the Bears?"*.

Here are some of the good openers I have seen or helped to develop:

Example 1:

"I want you to think differently about blood pressure. When the doctor or nurse takes yours, they express it in two numbers,

one over the other...systolic over diastolic. My research suggests that what matters most is the systolic pressure, that's the top number, and the difference between the two, known as the pulse pressure. Let me show you the evidence. First, let me explain why I think this can help all physicians who are faced with hypertensive patients..."

Example 2:

"Einstein said that the key to solving a problem was first to define it correctly." So, there was much excitement when the Harvard professor, Judah Folkman, first worked out how tumours attract blood vessels so they can take nutrients from the body to allow them to grow and eventually spread. He called the process angiogenesis. That sounded pretty cool, as it defined the problem, which was then, "'How can we prevent angiogenesis? How difficult can that be?" Well, that was in 1971 and we haven't solved it yet. The problem was far more complex than we thought, because angiogenesis is really clever and involves a number of different processes. You cut off one, and others take up the slack. Our new type of drug aims to cut them all off at the same time..."

Example 3:

"When I was a child, we thought that in the future, space travel would be commonplace, most menial tasks would be carried out by robots, and nobody would die of disease because we would have a cure for everything. As we know, it didn't turn out like that...at least, not yet. I don't know what happened to the rockets and the robots, but disease and serious illness are definitely still with us. The problem is, we don't have enough money to treat all the people who need it. Resources are precious. So I want to start my talk with a question: Why should we give liver transplants to alcoholics, lung transplants to smokers, and perform cardiac surgery on people who refuse to lose weight? Isn't it a waste of those precious resources? No,

it isn't. I want to talk about exactly why we should do those things, because that's why we have a National Health Service..."

All these intros are attention-grabbing. They're also relevant to the audience, and provide a lead into the main topic. You need to work out your own openers, those which are appropriate to you and your audiences.

In Part 1 I introduced 'The Grid' method of planning a talk. It included the advice to 'Start strong and finish strong' Here are the three strong endings from those talks:

Example 1:

So. I hope that in the last 20 minutes I've encouraged you to think differently about blood pressure. I hope I've demonstrated that the systolic pressure is what matters, rather than the traditional fraction of systolic over diastolic, and that the difference between the two, known is pulse pressure, is a good indicator of cardiovascular health. Now we have a few minutes for questions....'

Example 2:

"I set out today to show you that angiogenesis is far more complicated than we thought when it was first identified 44 years ago. We now know it involves three main processes which can all compensate for the others... so it is necessary to block all three of them to have a chance of preventing tumour growth. Our new compound is the first one to block all three. There's still a long way to go, but I hope you can see why we believe it offers promise in the treatment of solid tumours. Now we have time for questions....'

Example 3:

"To summarise...there is much debate about where to invest

the precious resources of our health services. It's sometimes claimed that they should not be spent on patients who have, in some people's minds, only themselves to blame for their health problems. I don't believe we should divide people into the 'guilty sick' and the 'innocent sick'. I believe everyone is deserving of the best service we can provide. That's why I became a doctor. I hope you agree with me and I'd be happy to discuss this further in the time we have left....'

Some time ago I was asked to be the moderator of a conference on HIV and AIDS in Geneva, Switzerland. The audience comprised of a varied group, including HIV/AIDS support groups, physicians, scientists, fundraisers, the Bill & Melinda Gates Foundation, UN Aids and representatives from large pharmaceutical companies. While there's much these groups agree on, there's also a lot of fundamental disagreement between some of them, so I knew I had to set the scene correctly at the start. I wanted to inspire them and emphasise the points that united them rather than those which set them apart.

After welcoming them, thanking them for coming and introducing myself as a medical journalist from London, I said:

"Before I move on to the agenda I'd like to tell you a story. 25 years ago I was a TV journalist in London covering what we then called the AIDS epidemic. That was the language we used. I'm sure you all remember the tombstone ads in the UK, when it seemed the whole population thought we would all die of AIDS. I interviewed a leading professor (who I identified and was known to the audience) at the time, and he said, 'If you get a diagnosis of HIV today, choose the wood for your coffin, and don't start any long books. It's a death sentence.' Yet now, 25 years later, if two people are diagnosed ... one with HIV and the other with diabetes, the one with HIV has every chance of living longer than the one with diabetes. That's how far we've come. That progress is thanks to the people, organisations and companies in this room. The reason we're here together is to ensure we continue that progress and start to make inroads against this terrible disease."

During the coffee break and over lunch, several people commented on my opening story. They remarked that how interesting it is that we rarely look back at our progress because we're so focused on where we need to go. I told that story because two weeks earlier I'd seen a report in a medical journal stating that people with HIV now have a life expectancy similar to the rest of the population. The report was full of detail, acronyms, numbers, and footnotes. Here is an extract from that report:

First the good news: People with HIV may enjoy life spans close to normal if they are on antiretroviral therapy, maintain low viral loads and CD4 counts above 350, are not coinfected with viral hepatitis, and are not injection drug users, according to a new study from the United Kingdom, aidsmap reports. Furthermore, those who survive past 60 may have life expectancies that surpass normal, thanks to better overall health care.

The projections on life expectancy derive from the UK Collaborative HIV Cohort (UK CHIC) which is a database of 43,000 patient records collected from 20 of the UK's largest HIV clinics. UK CHIC's Margaret May, PhD, examined mortality data concerning people who began taking anti-retrovirals after the ago of 20 between 2000 and 2008, and tracked them until 2010. As data points, the study took each patient's CD4 count and viral load just before they started therapy and compared them with the last CD4 and viral load figures for each subsequent year.
Final results were expressed as the number of subsequent years a patient could expect to live past his or her 35th birthday. The study excluded injection drug users.

Fig 3.1

That is data. My opening remarks turned it into a story. It's important to realise that without the data there wouldn't have been a story. Too often in presentations there's data but no story.

Why did that story work? Why did it strike a chord with the audience? Why did it have the unifying effect that I'd hoped for when I decided to tell it? The first reason is that it had *relevance*. Relevance is a huge element in storytelling and should be front and centre of all your presentations. I was a journalist for many years, and in the news business, relevance is the trump card. My favourite definition of news centres on this concept of relevance:

News is anything that makes people think, 'That could be me.'

Relevance is why anti-smoking campaigns which focus on your risk of lung cancer in later life, fail with school kids who are taking up the habit. It's also the reason why young ex-heroin addicts and ex-prisoners are likely to be more successful than Police officers at warning school kids about the dangers of drug addiction. We listen to people who are like us, or have similar experiences, or in the case of the school kids, are like someone we might become. Thanks to *relevance,* we *relate* to them. Stories can help your audience to relate to you.

The second point is that my story had an *objective*. I told the story to have a particular effect, ie to make people think, and realise how far we've come in the fight against HIV/AIDS. This is a very important element of storytelling. It must have an aim. Stand up comedians tell stories to make people laugh. Your stories may also make them laugh, but you need a different ending in mind.   Stories are immensely powerful. They can move people to tears or to action. The right story can make people proud, sad, determined, angry, empowered, cheated, strong or weak, or many other things. When you decide to tell a story, be clear about what you want it to achieve.

The reason the story succeeded was because it contained the three essential elements of storytelling:

Fig 3.2

The problem for most presenters is that they're stuck in the land of **inform.** There is little **engagement** and virtually no **inspiration.** Information alone is rarely inspiring. We need to add the other elements to be good storytellers and become great presenters. Note also that these three words are in overlapping ovals, not in a bulleted list. You don't go down the list, ticking off the words as you go. A great storyteller moves freely between all three concepts during their talk.

There are three other words which are important here:

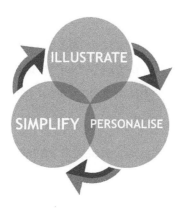

Fig 3.3

My story **illustrated** how far we've progressed with the treatment of HIV/AIDS. But I also **simplified** it hugely. I didn't talk about the different drug regimens, the problems of eating and sleeping, the stigma, or the problems of accessing supportive care at the time. I stripped the story down to its basics. I also **personalised** it. Personalisation is a two-way street. It means 'personal' to you as the presenter as well as to the audience. In this case, it meant involving myself and the audience in the story. I said, 'When I was a TV journalist...' which put me into the story. I then said that I'd interviewed a leading professor whose name they recognised. At that point I was stepping into their world, so we could both understand the significance of my story. Personalisation, as I discussed in Part 1, also involves relevance.

If you've followed my advice so far, you should be well on the way to becoming a competent and confident presenter. Your talks should be well-structured, have a beginning, a middle and an end, with a clear action point for the audience. They should be relevant and interesting, with just the right amount of detail. What does a story add to a talk that's missing from so many presentations?

The American poet and civil rights activist, Maya Angelou, summed it up beautifully:

'People will forget what you said,
people will forget what you did,
but people will never forget how you made them feel'

That's the essence of a good story. It makes people *feel*.

The Seven Basic Plots

It has been claimed, most notably by British author Christopher Booker, that although there are millions of stories, there are only seven basic plots. He worked for 34 years on his book

The Seven Basic Plots: Why We Tell Stories (published in 2004). He says all stories, whether from the Bible, Greek drama, Shakespeare or Hollywood, follow one of the plots. They are, with examples in brackets:

1. Overcoming the Monster (Perseus, Dracula, Jaws)

2. Rags to Riches   (David Copperfield, Cinderella, Harry Potter)

3. The Quest (The Odyssey, Lord of the Rings, Indiana Jones)

4. Voyage and Return (Gulliver's Travels, The Wizard of Oz, Back to the Future)

5. Comedy (A Midsummer Night's Dream, When Harry met Sally, Groundhog Day)

6. Tragedy (Anna Karenina, Romeo and Juliet, Breaking Bad)

7. Rebirth (Beauty and the Beast, A Christmas Carol, It's a Wonderful Life)

The idea is relevant in two ways: First, you can use the plots as storylines for your own talks. I'm sure that you can work out your own examples with a little thought. Here are some ways you could use the seven plots to tell your business or organisation's story:

1. *Overcoming the monster:* Any business that takes on a huge incumbent, as the 'challenger banks' have in the UK.

2. *Rags to Riches:* Any story that starts with one, usually poor, person with a great idea and builds into a great success. Used in Johnnie Walker Scotch or Grey Goose vodka.

3. *The Quest:* Any story involving a long search for perfection, cure or betterment, such as drug development or ecological improvements.

4. *Voyage and Return:* The theme here is that the voyage makes you a better/more successful person, or can help you find or develop something not available nearer home. Your story may be that you have had to travel to a challenging place to find components or elements of your product, or that going somewhere else made you think or see things differently.

5. *Comedy.* Hard to get right in a presentation, but there can be elements of humour, as discussed elsewhere in the book.

6. *Tragedy.* A common theme in medical presentations, where a new drug or procedure came too late to save someone. Use it sparingly, as you don't want to be accused of exploiting tragic situations.

7. *Rebirth.* Can be used to illustrate a change of brand or identity, eg when Marathon became Snickers, Andersen Consulting became Accenture, or Datsun became Nissan. Also useful for telling merger and acquisition stories.

The second point of relevance to your presentations is that all the plots, and all successful stories, make people *feel.* Your story-led talks should do the same. Stories engage the emotions in a way that cannot be achieved by a cold list of facts. I experience this regularly when I see or hear a great storyteller. Driving to work this morning I was listening to immunologist Professor Sheena Cruickshank talk about the human immune system. To her, it's the site of a constant battle between the 'alien invaders' such as viruses, bacteria or fungi, and the 'border guards' whose job is to keep them out. Her enthusiasm was infectious as she talked about 'lines of defence' and 'calls to arms' when the barriers are breached. She used phrases like 'blast holes in cells' and 'gobble them up' to describe complicated scientific processes. She humanised the enemies of the immune system and painted great word pictures, describing toxiplasma gondii as 'a brilliant parasite' that featured in the movie *Trainspotting*.

Listening to her I felt excited at the progress being made by her and other scientists, sorrow as she told us how her brother's death from cancer was what sparked her interest in the subject, pride that she's a British scientist who is leading the world with her research, and frustration that people like her are not better-known and rewarded in our celebrity-obsessed society. I said earlier that a story is like a Trojan Horse, sneaking messages into the citadel of the human mind. Prof. Cruickshank's talk was a great example of that. By the end I had learned more about the immune system, but it felt like I'd been told a good story. You can listen to her here: https://www.bbc.co.uk/programmes/b0b50kwx

A good story appeals to people in a more visceral way than a cold recitation of facts. Listen to any historian telling you why they took up that particular subject and the chances are they had a teacher who made history come alive. They told them stories rather than just handing out lists of dates. Scientists were inspired by motivational scientists telling stories. We can do the same in our presentations. A good story is:

- Engaging

- Authentic

- Creative

- Impactful

- Inspirational

- Memorable

It establishes a personal and emotional connection with the audience. An increasing body of scientific research demonstrates that the human brain processes stories differently from facts and data. Stories that are personal and emotionally compelling engage more of the brain, and thus are better remembered than simply a set of facts.

A good story can inspire action. It takes people on a journey. It's like the difference between travelling long haul in economy, where you endure a crushed, uncomfortable ride that just gets you from A to B, and the enjoyable, memorable experience of business or first class. Always aim to give your audience business class, at least!

However, a word of caution: Mastering storytelling techniques needs work. Just as my storytelling seminar can't turn you into an ace storyteller in a day, neither can this book. I can set you on the road, give you practical techniques and ideas. I hope I can inspire you to go out and find your own stories, try them out on different audiences and adapt as necessary. But without your ideas, your input and your investment of time, you won't make it as a storyteller. You also need to be comfortable with the techniques.

I urge you to try out. Above all, you need to practise, and as you do so, improve. It won't be plain sailing, and just like with any new skill, you'll make mistakes. The key is to learn from them, get back out there and try again. I constantly try out new stories in my presentations. Some work well, others less so. If something doesn't work, I try to analyse the reasons why, and then I might modify it or drop it all together.

Storytelling down the ages

The idea of storytelling is not new. It dates back more than 3,000 years and was a key element of **Rhetoric.** For centuries, scholars have argued over the true meaning and definition of rhetoric, and there's lots of information in the usual sources if you want to find out more. For our purposes, I offer you the words attributed to Aristotle, generally accepted as the first master of the subject. He called it *'the faculty of observing in any given case the available means of persuasion.'* In this case he meant 'observing' as in 'using' or 'following' as in 'observing the rules'. Another definition refers to rhetoric as *'The art of discourse, wherein a writer or speaker strives to inform, persuade or motivate particular audiences in specific situations.'*

Note the references to *persuasion.* Today, some companies and organisations are uncomfortable with this idea, believing it to be unethical in some way. That depends on how you use it. If a doctor persuades a patient to take regular exercise, stop smoking or take their medicine, that's a good thing. That's how we use it, as a force for good, and that's how it was originally designed. From Ancient Greece to the early 20th century, it was a central part of Western education. An educated man (women didn't engage in public life back then) was expected to speak and write persuasively. The study of rhetoric was the key to doing so. According to Aristotle, there are three modes of persuasion which must be used in the right balance to convince audiences. He called them 'artistic proofs,' and they are:

Aristotle's artistic proofs

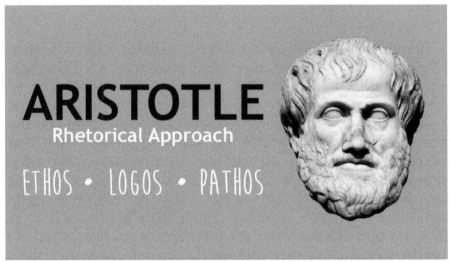

Fig 3.4

Ethos

Ethos is the Greek word for *character*. It gives us the modern word *ethics* or *ethical* and refers to your standing in the community. It's a combination of your reputation, experience, qualifications, learning and seniority. Most people who are asked to present at conferences have lots of ethos, otherwise they wouldn't have been invited. As a presenter, you may seek to establish your ethos quickly at the start of your talk, to demonstrate your credentials. I sometimes start a presentation on communication by showing pictures of the books I've written on the subject. This is not boasting. It's simply a quick way of establishing my own *ethos* with the audience. Given that my audiences are usually comprised of scientists and doctors who respect publication and the written word, showing them my books is usually well-received. However, if I was talking to a media audience I might refer to the awards I've won for making documentaries, or my time as a news journalist.

I saw an unusual example of *ethos* at an awards dinner in London. The audience was comprised of sales and marketing professionals from pharmaceutical companies. The host and guest speaker was the well-known, popular British comedian, John Bishop. He was a surprise guest, and when he came on he was greeted with enthusiasm. Then he said, *"It's great to be here tonight, not just because I like being with 1,000 people who are all having a great time and I can tell you a few jokes. But also because I know what you do. In fact, before I became a full-time comedian, I did what you do. I was a sales rep for a drug firm. I have carried the bag.".*

The audience went wild. He'd revealed himself to be 'one of them.' From that moment, he could do no wrong. He did this very cleverly, by using one of 'their' phrases, 'I have carried the bag.' which had a special resonance for that specific audience. (Traditionally, it referred to the bag of demo samples the sales rep carried on visits to physicians). This is an important element of the establishment of *ethos*. Using the right language is a quick way to do it.

Another way to achieve it is to find common ground with your audience. We tend to trust people who are similar to us. One of the greatest demonstrations of this was by Winston Churchill. In December 1941, just three weeks after the Japanese attack on Pearl Harbor, he was given the rare honour of being invited to address both branches of Congress. He was given a rousing reception, and began his by stressing his own American roots, immediately establishing common ground with his hosts:

"Members of the Senate and of the House of Representatives of the United States, I feel greatly honored that you should have thus invited me to enter the United States Senate Chamber and address the representatives of both branches of Congress. The fact that my American forebears have for so many generations played their part in the life of the United States, and that here I am, an Englishman, welcomed in your midst, makes this experience one of the most moving and thrilling in my life, which is already long and has not been entirely uneventful.

I wish indeed that my mother, whose memory I cherish across the vale of years, could have been here to see. By the way, I cannot help reflecting that if my father had been American and my mother British, instead of the other way around, I might have got here on my own."

This light-hearted remark brought laughter and cheers to the sombre occasion and left the US politicians in no doubt about the relevance of the British Prime Minister and the serious matter he was about to address. It was also a good example of personalising his story. He was saying, in effect, 'The war may seem a long way away but, take my word for it, it could be your turn next.'

Logos

Logos gives us the modern word *logic*. It refers to a scientific rationale or logical argument leading to a logical conclusion. It can be based on a range of factors, including:

- Data
- Facts
- Statistics
- Studies
- Examples
- History
- Evidence
- Demonstrations

However, it's rarely sufficient to rely solely on *logos*. Some presentations miss the target because the presenter believes they can persuade the audience with just the facts alone. You can't, which is why skilled barristers and attorneys command such high fees. They understand perfectly the relationship between *ethos, logos* and *pathos*.. The facts alone rarely speak for themselves. Aristotle believed that people are fundamentally reasonable and are capable of making decisions based on what makes the most sense. 'Persuasion occurs through the arguments when we show the truth or the apparent truth from whatever is persuasive in each case.' You need clear, concise and logical arguments to provide substance to your message.

In general, you can develop strong *logos* by following three general principles:

1. Make it Understandable

Whatever arguments you use, they must be easily understood by the audience before they can be persuasive. There are two elements to understanding: the *concepts* and the *language*. You need to ensure your audience can understand both. This means matching the level of complexity to the audience. For outstanding examples of this, see the annual announcements of the Nobel Prize winners at www.nobelprize.org. The site contains different versions of the science that won the physics, chemistry and medicine awards headed 'popular information' and 'advanced information.' This is a great example of what I call 'Lego v Duplo' approach:

Lego is a great and creative toy for children aged about three and upwards. However, the children need quite sophisticated motor skills to handle and use the intricately-designed small bricks, and mature conceptual thinking to plan the creations. The makers of Lego realised this, so they launched Duplo, a simpler version of Lego, with bigger pieces, bright colours and easier fixings. It's suitable for younger children who at that stage lack the development, sophistication or understanding of their older friends and siblings.

Communication, and presentations in particular, are the same – some audiences can handle the Lego version because they have sufficient understanding and skills. Others know less or are peripherally involved in the subject, so they need the Duplo variant. The analogy works well in other areas too. For example, I have recently been working with a company who are making some people redundant. Those whose jobs are being eliminated want and deserve to know all the details, including how they can apply for new jobs in the company and what their severance pay they can expect. They need the Lego version. Those who are not affected, however, only need the big picture, ie the Duplo version. I urge you to think about your own presentations in this way.

2. Make it Logical

Make sure your arguments stand up to a range of pressures, from simple cynicism to detailed forensic examination. This doesn't mean you have to include all the details, just that you've thought it all through. The best way to do this is to stress-test it verbally with a colleague. Make sure your arguments don't have holes in them.

For example, I was working with a pharmaceutical client who was about to report a shortage of a key drug. They said they couldn't make enough of it, so were recommending patients switch to a different drug, which was more expensive. Critics claimed the company didn't really have production problems at all, but were just trying to move patients onto the more expensive product. The usual drug is produced in what's called an IV formulation, meaning it's administered in hospital by an intravenous drip. The company said they couldn't make enough of it, but they could make the newer version, which would be self-injected by patients at home. In the message development session, I said, "The essential ingredient of both these products is the same, yes? You say that's what you can't get hold of. So you can't make the IV version, yet you can make the more expensive newer one? Why don't you use your rare ingredients to make the older, cheaper drug instead?"'

It was a key point in the preparation session, provoked a deeper investigation into the causes and revealed a different position entirely. This, in turn, led to a completely different line of argument, which was broadly accepted even by the company's critics. If they had gone out with the original argument, they would have failed on the *logos.*

Making a logical argument is even more critical, and more difficult than ever, in the current environment of 'post-truth' and 'alternative facts. The US President says that global warming isn't the result of human activity, despite the scientific evidence, and when asked about the alleged poisoning of an ex-Russian agent in the UK said, 'We're going to wait for the facts. If we accept them, we'll condemn it.' The idea that you might just not accept the facts is a frightening one, but does illustrate the challenge – and importance - of establishing a logical argument.

3. Make it Real

An argument is comprised of a number of premises, leading to a conclusion. If your premises are based on specific facts and examples, they're more likely to be accepted than those which are abstract and general. The more easily your premises are accepted, the more easily your conclusions will be as well.

Pathos

Pathos is derived from the Greek word for *suffering* or *experience.* It gives us the modern words *empathy* or *sympathy* and refers to the way you establish an emotional connection with the audience. It is often misunderstood, and erroneously taken to mean that your talk must contain an emotional story that makes an audience laugh or cry. It can be that, but it also means, for example, painting a memorable word picture, appropriate humour, a vivid description or even an engaging delivery. Passion and enthusiasm are elements of *pathos.*

It means stirring your audience into action by connecting to their emotions. The emotion can be fear, anger, sorrow, pride, sympathy, or any other. The key element is that you need to know the emotion you want to provoke, and what you want your audience to do with it. So if you're speaking on behalf of cancer patients who can't afford their drugs, you may make the audience angry. But the point of your talk must be to get them to do something with that anger. You might want them to lobby their politicians, go on a march, sign a petition, vote for change or donate money...all these are valid objectives. The point is:

- You need to know which emotion you're trying to provoke

- You need to tell them what to do with the emotion.

Politicians speaking about the plight of rough sleepers, refugees or civilian victims of wars are relying largely on *pathos*.

Martin Luther King relied on *pathos* in his *I have a dream...* speech:

"I am not unmindful that some of you have come here out of great trials and tribulations. Some of you have come fresh from narrow jail cells. And some of you have come from areas where your quest -- quest for freedom left you battered by the storms of persecution and staggered by the winds of police brutality. You have been the veterans of creative suffering. Continue to work with the faith that unearned suffering is redemptive. Go back to Mississippi, go back to Alabama, go back to South Carolina, go back to Georgia, go back to Louisiana, go back to the slums and ghettos of our northern cities, knowing that somehow this situation can and will be changed."

People sometimes ask me which of the three elements of rhetoric is the most important. My answer is that they're all important and that a good persuasive speech contains elements of all three. However, you need the right amount of each. The 'right amount' will vary depending on your audience, topic and objectives.

There is, however, one element that never varies: you always want your *ethos* to be as high as possible. There's no such thing as too much credibility. When it comes to logos and pathos, however, you'll want to adjust the amount of each, depending on the subject and the audience.

Storytelling targets

Aristotle was not the only citizen of the ancient world whose rules we still follow in presentations. Nearly 300 years later. Cicero was an eminent politician and lawyer in Ancient Rome. He was regarded as the greatest orator of his day, and wrote that the perfect orator had three key attributes:

Docere: Knowledge of how to inform the audience in a manner that holds their attention.

Delectare: Knowledge of how to charm an audience with expansive, pleasant narratives or playful wit.

Flectere: Knowledge of how to inflame various emotions.

When you consider the great speakers of today, don't you think it's notable that they exhibit the same skills?

In terms of storytelling in the modern world, I think of three similar targets:

Fig 3.5

The head responds to logos and to ethos. It responds to intellectual, rational, logical arguments and also to the speaker's reputation and expertise. **The heart** brings in the *pathos,* the emotional, empathetic or sympathetic elements of an argument. They are straightforward. **Gut instinct** is less easy to define. It refers to the instinctive reaction we have when we see, hear or meet somebody. Gut instinct is based on intuition, which itself is probably based partly on experience. There's a body of academic research which suggests our gut instincts are better than our brains at spotting conmen and fraudsters, or a feeling that someone isn't being honest with us. The question is whether you can affect this at all. The answer is, 'Yes, of course you can.' You can do this in a number of ways. The key one is with the words you use. Just as non-native English speakers often make tiny errors in their English and reveal their non-English origins, your words will give you away.

We see it in both our personal and professional lives. It's a common misconception that a sub-editor on a newspaper is an assistant editor. It's not, and anyone using the phrase in that way shows they don't understand journalism or newspapers. I remember, some time ago, a man who I got to know socially realised that I'm a big soccer fan, and claimed that he was, too. The next time I saw him he referred to a previous score as 'two-love.' That's a tennis score! Nobody uses 'love' to mean nil or zero in a soccer match. My gut instinct told me he was bull******ng. Recently I saw a senior PR person presenting to an international group of pharmaceutical executives. At one point she was talking about the political bias of various UK newspapers. She described the London *Evening Standard* as 'a typical Tory paper.' This was not true. The Editor is (at the time of writing) the former UK Chancellor of the Exchequer (Finance Minister) George Osborne. He was sacked from the Government by Prime Minister Theresa May, resigned as an MP and took on the *Standard* job. He has used the job as a platform to regularly attack his old adversary, Mrs. May, particularly on her stance on Brexit. He's even described her politically as 'a dead woman walking.' So, although it's still a broadly conservative-supporting newspaper, it's far from being a 'typical Tory paper.' When the presenter said it, my gut instinct told me she didn't know what she was talking about on that subject and I was sceptical about everything else she said. Essentially, she'd lost her ethos.

If you claim to be a specialist in something, you need to be able to talk the talk. For example, I often use a quote attributed to Einstein: *'Make things as simple as possible, but no simpler'*. I always say that it's 'attributed to Einstein' because I can't find any evidence that he said it (in any language). It's quite feasible that the quote is (ironically, given its subject) a simplification of this:

"It can scarcely be denied that the supreme goal of all theory is to make the irreducible basic elements as simple and as few as possible without having to surrender the adequate representation of a single datum of experience."

We know he said these words during The Herbert Spencer Lecture, delivered at Oxford in June 1933. It is well-referenced, so I'm comfortable quoting him. In some presentations, I use that quote as well, when I think the audience will appreciate (or even demand) it. Given that I work mainly in a scientific or medical environment, where facts and references are the cornerstone of research, and a reputation for accuracy is key, these are important points. I do the same with the Mehrabian research about the importance of body language which I quoted in the first section of the book. I'm trying to influence the gut instincts of the individuals in the audience in my favour. Note that a gut instinct is unique to individuals, and therefore an audience cannot have one. You can, however, aim to influence the individual gut instincts of every person in the audience!

The challenge of gut instinct is that it happens almost immediately. You can influence it by the way you dress, smile, listen and speak. Even the way you approach the stage is important. In western societies, looking someone in the eye suggests trustworthiness (though in some cultures it signifies a challenge). A refusal to do this often suggests a lack of honesty. All these things feed into what we call gut instinct, so you need to be aware of it. There's more on this in the section on body language.

Put yourself in their shoes

As I outlined in Part 1, a key attribute of a good presenter is the ability to put themselves in the audience's shoes. Understanding the different appeals to the head, heart and gut will help you to do this. For example, if I'm addressing a group of Nobel Prize winners I'd expect them to respond primarily to a logical, rational argument, and would tailor my talk accordingly. I'd be appealing to the head, and using what Aristotle called an appeal to ethos and logos. However, with this I'd also use a little bit of emotion – a touch of pathos - to turn my information into a story. However, I need to get the balance right. It's like baking a cake with spices...too much, and it will be overspiced and ruined, too little and it will be bland. It's rather like injecting a tiny drop of food colouring into a jug of plain water. You don't need much to make an impression. As with food colouring, a dash of emotion goes a long way with such an audience.

A good example of this is the Nobel presentation by Bruce Beutler, an American immunologist and geneticist. Together with Jules A. Hoffmann, he received the 2011 Nobel Prize in Physiology for Medicine, for 'their discoveries concerning the activation of innate immunity.' He opened his Nobel lecture, marking his prize, with a photograph of his father, Ernest Beutler, MD, saying:

"I want to start with acknowledgement of my father because he was a great teacher of mine. He was not only a great scientist but also a great teacher, and we had hundreds of thousands of

discussions about science. I remember speaking with him about the innate immunity of plants when I was a child, maybe 10 or 12 years old. On a trip to sequoia trees in California, I asked him why the giant Redwood trees around us didn't just rot and disappear.

And we talked about the blights in potatoes and wheat, and we concluded that probably the plants did have some kind of active immunity.

It turned out – though I could never have imagined it at the time – that they do have a kind of immunity that related to the type that we have as mammals..."

The rest of his lecture was about the science of microbes and our immune system. He had just the right amount of pathos at the start of his talk.

The converse is also true. If I talk to a group of artists or other creative people I expect them to respond better to an emotional argument aimed at the heart and based on pathos. However with this audience, a little logic or rationalisation will also help to turn the presentation into a story with substance.

I like the analogy of the rider and the elephant originally presented by psychologist Jonathan Haidt in his book, *'The Happiness Hypothesis.'* (http://www. happinesshypothesis.com. He argues that we have two sides:

- An analytical/controlled/rational side (the rider).

- An emotional/automatic/irrational side (the elephant)

According to the model, the rider is rational and can plan ahead, while the elephant is irrational and driven by emotion and instinct. We have to find the balance between the two. This metaphor was developed further by Chip & Dan Heath in their book, *'Switch: How to Change When Change is Hard'*:

"Perched atop the elephant, the rider holds the reins and seems to be the leader. But the rider's control is precarious because the rider is so small relative to the elephant. Anytime the six-ton elephant and the rider disagree about which direction to go, the rider is going to lose. He's completely overmatched".

We can use the same metaphor to illustrate putting ourselves in the shoes of the audience: We need to keep the rider in control, but also remember the elephant has its needs.

Exercise 4

Think of a good presenter you've seen, who's a good storyteller. Look up some TED talks if nobody comes to mind. Analyse the way they use *ethos, logos* and *pathos,* and how they appeal to the head, the heart and the gut. Take a look at how they approach the stage, and how they start their talk. Ask yourself: Can I do something similar?

Storytelling techniques

What did your analysis reveal? What are the common attributes great presenters share? They were probably engaging, relaxed, confident, authoritative and made an instant connection with the audience. Their talk probably had a theme and a structure. However, many of these traits are a *consequence* of being good storytellers, rather than a *cause*. In this section I'm going to outline specific storytelling techniques that will improve your storytelling skills. These are the techniques I use regularly or see in other great presenters. The list isn't exhaustive, and you can always find more and better ways to make an impression. If you're a good storyteller, you may already be using some of them. Also note that some of the techniques overlap and/or can be combined, that not all will appeal to everyone, and all are to be used appropriately (that word again!). I do hope, however, that they'll assist you in broadening your techniques and go some way towards freeing your inner storyteller!

Using contrast, repetition and questions

Storytelling technique #1:
Contrast, repetition and questions

Contrast is a vital element of many of the arts. Composers use techniques such as bridges and counterpoint to emphasise the contrast within a piece of music. They change the pace to engage and surprise us. The sound of different sections or individual instruments in an orchestra is another illustration of the power of contrast. In the visual arts, photographers and artists deliberately put contrasting colours together, based on where they sit on the colour wheel. The appeal of some of the most memorable photographs and paintings is based on contrast, either in subject matter (the homeless person begging outside the opera) or in light (a bright sun rising over a dark landscape). Authors and documentary makers use juxtaposition, a way of placing two or more ideas, places, characters or actions, side by side to develop and accentuate comparisons and contrasts.

We should use the same idea – contrast – as an essential part of our presentations.

At the heart of every dull presentation is a lack of contrast, a lack of light and shade, or variety

This applies in almost all the elements of a talk, particularly all three legs of the stool – content, voice and body language. Such presentations have come to be called 'Death by PowerPoint,' and can send audiences into what Dilbert, the corporate cartoon character, calls a 'PowerPoint Coma.' They don't have a beginning, a middle and an end. They just start, go on (and on...and on...and on...) and eventually, stop. Monotone and monochrome are their watchwords.

Deliberate repetition, and the use of questions, are the close relations of contrast. This section introduces them all and illustrates how great speakers use them.

Contrast

We can use contrast in a number of ways. For example.

Language

Speech

Visuals

Content

Vocal style

Body language

Language

Contrast in language is one of the most powerful forms of communication and works just as well in fiction as in non-fiction. Here's the opening paragraph of the novel *A Tale of Two Cities* by Charles Dickens:

'It was the **best** of times, it was the **worst** of times,

it was the age of **wisdom**, it was the age of **foolishness**,

it was the epoch of **belief**, it was the epoch of **incredulity**,

it was the season of **light**, it was the season of **darkness**,

it was the spring of **hope,** it was the winter of **despair...**'

x

114

I hope you agree that the language in that excerpt is beautiful and powerful. Look at the contrast between best and worst, wisdom and foolishness, beliefs and incredulity, light and darkness, hope and despair. There's a rhythm to that language which makes it powerful and memorable.

President Kennedy is rightly regarded as one of the most eloquent orators of the 20th century. Many of his most memorable lines are based on contrast:

"Ask not what your country can do for you. Ask what you can do for your country."

"Mankind must put an end to war before war puts an end to mankind,"'

"Too often we... enjoy the comfort of opinion without the discomfort of thought."

Most of us, of course, will never reach the literary heights of JFK or Charles Dickens. We'll never reach the performance heights of Federer, Messi or Clapton either, but that doesn't stop us from being inspired by them.

Ideas stand or fail based on how they're conveyed. Stories are a great vehicle for doing this. However, they're not composed of ideas, but words, the common currency of communication. The words, the language we use, the phrases and sentences, are all key to the success of our ideas. Look at this short video to see a great example of how changing the words, but keeping the message the same, can make a huge difference to the outcome:

https://www.youtube.com/watch?v=Hzgzim5m7oU

Speech

Speech, of course, is spoken language. A presentation is comprised of spoken words, so let's look at a few examples where language in speech has been based on contrast, and the impact it's had. President John F Kennedy knew the value of using contrast in speech:

"We choose to go to the moon and do the other things in this decade, not because they are easy, but because they are hard. because that challenge is one that we are willing to accept, one we are unwilling to postpone, and one we intend to win .."

The technique of contrast overlaps with repetition. Repetition of keywords is another very powerful storytelling or presentation technique, as can be seen in the use of willing/unwilling. If you look at the full version of Kennedy's speech you'll see many examples of repetition and contrast. For example:

"We meet at a college noted for knowledge, in a city noted for progress, in a state noted for strength."

Once again, as in the case of Charles Dickens, there's a beautiful rhythm to Kennedy's speech, created by contrast and the repetition. Also note how he widens the circle of reference and relevance from the college, to the city and eventually the state. He also uses another technique: He goes on to spike his opponents' guns with a rhetorical flourish, portraying them as uninspired dullards with no imagination:

"But why, some say, the Moon? Why choose this as our goal? And they may well ask, why climb the highest mountain? Why, 35 years ago, fly the Atlantic? Why does Rice play Texas?" [He was speaking at Rice University in Texas.]

Other examples from JFK include:

"Let every nation know, whether it wishes us well or ill, that we shall pay any price, bear any burden, meet any hardship,

support any friend, oppose any foe to assure the survival and the success of liberty."

For a masterclass in the use of contrast and repetition, and an analysis of the speech, see: https://en.wikipedia.org/wiki/We_choose_to_go_to_the_Moon

Britain's wartime leader, Winston Churchill, was another of the world's greatest orators. His speech is littered with rhetorical devices, including contrast and repetition:

"This is not the end. It is not even the beginning of the end. But it is the end of the beginning."

"We shall go on to the end. We shall fight in France, we shall fight on the seas and oceans, we shall fight with growing confidence and growing strength in the air, we shall defend our island, whatever the cost may be. We shall fight on the beaches, we shall fight on the landing grounds, we shall fight in the fields and in the streets, we shall fight in the hills; we shall never surrender."

Look at the repetition of the phrase '100 years later' in Martin Luther King's 'I have a dream' speech, given 100 years after Abraham Lincoln signed the Emancipation Declaration, officially ending slavery in the US:

"But one hundred years later, the Negro still is not free. One hundred years later, the life of the Negro is still sadly crippled by the manacles of segregation and the chains of discrimination. One hundred years later, the Negro lives on a lonely island of poverty in the midst of a vast ocean of material prosperity. One hundred years later, the Negro is still languished in the corners of American society and finds himself in exile in his own land. So we have come here today to dramatise a shameful condition."

Also note how the juxtaposition of '100 years ago' and 'here today' brings up the reason for being here, while 'today' gives urgency.

Visual contrast

It is said that a picture paints a thousand words. It can also save you a lot of time and words in a presentation and lead you to tell great stories. Here's a graphic which clearly illustrates the difference in size and complexity between different kinds of drugs:

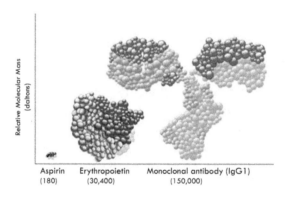

Fig 3.7

If you're aiming to show how developing, producing, storing, transporting and delivering IgG1 is far more complex than aspirin, the visual contrast here illustrates it clearly. However, with a more general audience, you may need to use another visual to make the same point:

Fig 3.8

THE PRESENTER'S SECRET WEAPON

Contrast in content

Contrast in content is one of the most powerful ways of presenting an argument. It's power lies in the fact that you're aiming to change someone's perception of the facts. This often involves putting the facts into a previously unconsidered context. Here are some ways you can use this technique:

Contrast the past with the present.

Tell a story which illustrates the now/then contrast. I used it earlier in the book when I introduced 'The Grid' method of planning a talk. My chosen subject was electric vehicles, and I began my talk with this statement:

"I've been researching and developing electric vehicles for more than 20 years...and what a change! When I started, it meant golf carts and milk floats. Now it means Tesla and Porsche.".

Facebook's Chief Operating Officer, Sheryl Sandbrook, won high praise for her 'Class Day' keynote address to graduating students at Harvard Business School (HBS) in 2012. Back in 1995 she told them she had been sitting where they are now. Then she used the contrast technique:

"It wasn't really that long ago when I was sitting where you are, but the world has changed an awful lot. My section, section B, tried to have HBS's first online class. We had to use an AOL chat room and dial up service. (Your parents can explain to you later what dial-up service is.) We had to pass out a list of screen names because it was unthinkable to put your real name on the internet. And it never worked. It kept crashing. The world just wasn't set up for 90 people to communicate at once online. But for a few brief moments, we glimpsed the

future – a future where technology would power who we are and connect us to our real colleagues, our real family, our real friends..

It used to be that in order to reach more people than you could talk to in a day, you had to be rich and famous and powerful. You had to be a celebrity, a politician, a CEO. But that's not true today. Now ordinary people have a voice, not just those of us lucky to go to HBS, but anyone with access to Facebook, Twitter, a mobile phone. This is disrupting traditional power structures and levelling traditional hierarchy. Control and power are shifting from institutions to individuals, from the historically powerful to the historically powerless. And all of this is happening so much faster than I could have imagined when I was sitting where you are today – and Mark Zuckerberg was 11 years old."

I saw another great example of this from a scientist working for a pharmaceutical company. His ten minute talk to an audience of non-scientists working for the same company, was a model of storytelling. He explained a complex scientific process very simply by using the appropriate language for the audience and translating his work into realistic, relevant examples. He took the audience with him, made it understandable and relevant to them (and their children) and started and ended with the same point. He accomplished all this by starting with an example of contrast:

"Hello, my name is Dr XYZ. When I was a kid I always wanted to be a scientist, and I imagined it meant wearing a white coat and doing experiments in a laboratory. Now I realise that science isn't really about that at all. That's where it starts, but it needs to come out of the lab into the real world, where it can help people. And what we have realised in recent times is that that process happens incredibly quickly. I want to show you an example of how that happens, and how the period between it being 'science' (as in, 'in a lab') and 'helpful' (in this case to people with cancer) is getting shorter all the time.

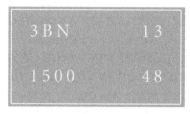

Fig 3.9

Any ideas what these figures represent? I want to talk about something called Next Generation Sequencing, or NGS. And it starts with the sequencing of the human genome. That's what these figures refer to. [Walks back to screen, and adds more information to the figures, so they now read:

Fig 3.10

The Human Genome Project was a gigantic international research programme to determine the sequence of the human genome and identify the genes that it contains. It cost three billion US Dollars, and took 13 years, with scientists all over the world contributing. That was how much it cost, and how long it took to sequence just one genome. Many people said, 'This is crazy.' And in one sense, it was. However, it was done with what we might call 'Last Generation Sequencing.

Look what's happened since then. Now we have NGS - Next Generation Sequencing. Look at the figures on the bottom row. If you want to get your genome sequenced, you can get it done for about 1000 US Dollars, and it will take about 48 hours. The cost and the time taken are coming down all the time. Soon, NGS will become part of everyday medical care for you, and your children.

I work on a project called ABC999. We are trying to use NGS as the basis for a test for cancer patients. When someone has cancer, many of their cells are compromised, or damaged, in a particular way. We are developing a test which, using NGS, can map each individual patient's genome. It will tell us if any of their cells are compromised in this specific way. We are also developing a drug that will, we hope, just target those specific cells, and repair that damage, without affecting the healthy cells around it. Hopefully, that will become a common way to treat cancer.

For the patient it's just a blood test. It's not even invasive, but the results could be life-saving, or life-changing."

He went into more detail, based mainly on biology and chemistry, which he explained very clearly, aware that he was talking to non-scientists. Then he moved on to the type of cancer patients the technology could help. To summarise, he walked back to the whiteboard and the figures.

"We are making an NGS application affordable and achievable in a realistic timeframe. I hope you can see the progression here: We start with programmes like this [Human Genome Project], which people say are crazy, unaffordable and will take years. But they spawn projects like this [NGS] which benefits patients like this [example of damaged gene]. That's what we do, and what I mean when I say science needs to get out of the laboratory and into the real world to help people. I hope this has been interesting and understandable, and I'd be delighted to take any questions."

This short talk happened about five years ago but has remained with me. He was a brilliant presenter (and a very clever scientist!). He smiled encouragingly, and my gut instinct was that he's a man who loves his job, is passionate about the possibilities of science, and is completely in command of his subject. He had maximum ethos, and his talk had the right balance of logos and pathos.

I said earlier that to be a good storyteller you need to be able to put yourself in the audience's shoes. To see how well this presenter did this, and as a contrast, look up NGS online. You will find scientific explanations which, though clear, lack impact. They are mainly comprised of *logos*, they appeal to logic, with virtually no *pathos* whatsoever. Here's an example from a company offering NGS:

Next generation sequencing (NGS) technology is revolutionising life sciences research and healthcare. The speed, throughput and flexibility of NGS provides researchers with the means to gain valuable insights at a rate never before possible. No longer used for purely academic research, NGS technologies are now spreading to clinical applications and helping to refine our understanding of disease.

There is nothing wrong with that example at all.. It's clear, succinct, and conveys the necessary information. It comes from a business-to-business (b2b) website. The company's potential customers don't need much pathos in the pitch. Both the website and the presentation are good examples of how clear communication is based on the needs of the audience.

The contrast is often most effective when the contrasting elements are placed next to one another. This is often achieved most simply when the two statistics don't need much elaboration.

"Cancer survival rates in the UK have doubled in the last 40 years."

"The number of people killed in road accidents in the UK has almost halved since the year 2000."'

"Thirty years ago people died from ulcers which needed potentially dangerous surgery. Now they take pills and are cured."

"Thirty years ago a Compaq portable computer weighed 18 pounds and had a 20Mb hard disk. Now an iPhone has 256Gigabytes and weighs six ounces."

"Twenty five years ago we hadn't even identified hepatitis C. Now it can be cured in 12 weeks with tablets."

"Rates of teenage pregnancy in the UK have halved in the past two decades and are now at their lowest levels since record-keeping began in the late 1960s."

Exercise 5

Using contrast, repetition and questions

Take a look at a recent presentation and try to find a place or places where you could use contrast, repetition and/or questions to illustrate your points and make your talk more memorable.

Create a memorable moment

Technique #2: Create a memorable moment

In this book I've quoted a number of presentations I've seen over the years. Some of them were many years ago, but they've stuck in my mind. I assume you're the same. Take a moment now to think about the best presentations you've seen. What was special about them? Obviously, as you remember them, they were, literally, memorable. That's our aim, of course. One way of being memorable is to create what I call a *memorable moment*. This gets to the heart of why we want to tell stories rather than just passing on information: to be memorable. We can achieve this in many ways and in this section I want to give you some examples. I've arranged them around a number of techniques which I hope will help you to work out your own versions. The list is not all-inclusive, but I hope will spur you on to find your own examples, based on your own style and area of expertise.

A surprising statistic

Numbers are a great way to get people's attention and make your case. There's a robustness to figures and statistics that's not always present in other forms of argumentation. I often use numbers at the start of a presentation, and the more surprising, the better. For example, I was asked to make a presentation to respiratory physicians in the Middle East region. The topic of my talk was whether, if we spoke differently to asthma patients, we could encourage them to use their inhalers correctly and cut the number of deaths and hospital admissions from within that patient group. [Note that I didn't say we need to *improve* the way we spoke to them. As I'm not a physician, I have no *ethos* when it comes to patient consultations. However, as a communication specialist, I have lots of it].

I opened my talk with this slide:

MEMORABLE MOMENT: STARTLING STATISTIC

GINA guidelines:
'Most asthma patients can avoid serious attacks and have near-normal lung function.'

The reality:
250,000 will die of asthma attacks this year

Why?

Fig 3.11

I said, *"I want to open my talk today with two questions. According to GINA, the global asthma guidelines, most asthma patients can avoid serious attacks and have near normal lung function. That's an aspiration. However the reality is that this year, a quarter of a million people will die of asthma attacks. Question one: How can these two things exist? Question two: If we talked to patients differently - if we changed the way we communicate with them - could we get them to use their asthma medication properly, and so improve outcomes? Or put simply, can we start to cut the number of asthma deaths and attacks?"*

Note the use of contrast, repetition and questions here, as well as surprising statistics!

Other examples of surprising statistics:

Every day, 18 people die waiting for an organ transplant.

Every 10 minutes a family is made homeless.

Dementia research gets 13 times less funding than cancer even though the cost to society is far greater, Oxford University has found. [Note the use of contrast and a statistic].

Statistics can be surprisingly small as well as surprisingly large. For example:

European governments spend less than three per cent of their budgets on preventing illness and disease.

A great quote

A great quote is memorable, poignant and pithy. It can also provide a theme to your talk. For example, I was making a presentation about the reputation of the pharmaceutical industry to a group of senior executives from drug firms. I wanted to call for a change in language and message, primarily about the cost of drugs and transparency in clinical trial data. I began with a picture of Albert Einstein and the quote attributed to him:

The definition of insanity is doing the same thing over and over again, and expecting a different result

I said, *"I've been working as a communication consultant to big drug firms for 25 years. Throughout that time we've tried to justify the cost of drugs by saying that research and development is very expensive, and we only have a short time to get a return on our investment before the patent expires, then anyone else can make it and the drugs are made available cheaply. Do you know what? They didn't believe us 25 years ago, and they still don't believe us today.*

We're falling into the Einstein trap. In fact, he would probably say we're insane. We constantly say the same thing, yet expect a different result. We have to change what we say and change what we do. I want to give you some examples.."

Another quote I've used to start a presentation was given to me from a well-known Professor of Dermatology, who said:

When I started practising medicine, dermatology was simple: If it's wet, dry it. If it's dry, wet it.

Now we have his amazing developments like monoclonal antibodies.

It's like immunology on the outside of the body.

I wish I was starting again today

Both the Einstein and dermatology quotes became the themes for my talks. The Internet is awash with great quotes...look them up and use them. But please, in the interests of accuracy, try and check who actually said it first (Mark Twain gets a lot of erroneous credit), and make sure it leads naturally into the point you want to make. I see many presenters who open with a memorable moment, such as a cartoon, drawing or a story, but then it doesn't lead anywhere. To me, this is like clickbait on the Internet... it's not fair on the audience and they'll be dissatisfied.

A personal story

This is one of the most powerful ways of engaging your audience. In fact it's so powerful that you have to be careful how, where and when you use it. I was once asked to give a talk at a European mental health support group. I opened it with a photograph of myself with my father and explained that he suffered from paranoid schizophrenia. After having the condition for many years he was diagnosed and received very effective treatment, which eliminated his symptoms and enabled him to live a near normal life, without paranoia. In my talk I described how, as a result of being given this drug, he was no longer putting blankets over the windows because he thought people were watching him, and had stopped unplugging the radio at night, which he used to do to prevent people listening to him.

The problem, I said, is that the drug had an unfortunate side effect. It made my father's hands very shaky, something called EPS. [Pause] My father was an amateur artist [pause] so shaky hands were a disaster for him. He knew the problem was caused by the drugs, so occasionally he would stop taking the tablets and pick up his painting equipment again. He would then suffer breakthrough symptoms of schizophrenia. "Wouldn't it be great," I ask the audience, "if the treatments for schizophrenia were as effective as that one, but without the unwanted side effects?" And that, I say, is exactly what is being developed now.

I've also used that story to illustrate that progress is being made against a number of very difficult-to-treat illnesses, but that progress doesn't necessarily mean a drug is more effective... it can mean it has fewer or less troublesome side effects. The way I told the story verbally was also a good example of how to use a pause for dramatic effect. Whenever I tell it now, I pause after revealing he was an artist, to let the implications of that resonate with the audience. I usually see the atmosphere change in the room to one of immense sympathy.

A personal story needs to fulfill a number of criteria to work with an audience. First, it needs to be authentic. Authenticity is a strange and wonderful thing. It's difficult to define, but easy to see. It involves appearing genuine and honest. Lack of authenticity is even easier to detect, thanks to the gut instinct I discussed earlier in this chapter. This means that your 'personal story' should have happened to you or somebody you know, or at least you need to be aware of the full circumstances surrounding it. Feel free to borrow stories from others, but be honest about their origins. You need to be very comfortable when telling your story and be sympathetic to the situation you're describing. It's a very personal thing; you have to feel that you are revealing something of yourself. Only you can decide whether you want to put yourself through that.

You also need to be ready to defend it. In one recent presentation I told the story of my father and his schizophrenia, as I often do. Given that the audience were diabetes specialists, I also talked about my stepdaughter and granddaughter who both suffer with diabetes. One member of the audience asked if I had a pocket full of pictures and stories concerning a range of medical conditions to suit every situation! I laughed and explained that these were my real family members. Other audience members laughed at his question, as they had (I assume) not queried my honesty in relating the story. It does illustrate, however, the need to be authentic. If they hadn't been my real relatives, I would have lost credibility and ethos.

Where do stories come from?

This leads me onto another question often asked at my storytelling seminars: where do I find stories?   The answer is that I try to keep my eyes and ears open and to be receptive to ideas. I'm genuinely interested in people, events, anecdotes, and am always on the lookout for stories I can share. Sometimes I just share them with friends, other times I put them in my talks. Sometimes I do both. I read a lot, listen and watch widely, and I have the mind of a typical journalist. ('A snapper-up of unconsidered trifles'). I see, read and hear things and store them away. Then something in my brain links to a point I want to make.

For example, a couple of days ago I read that Charlie Chaplin once came third in a Charlie Chaplin lookalike competition. I've been smiling about that ever since. (Apparently, the judges were confused by his bright blue eyes, which didn't show in black and white films). I've also learnt that Dolly Parton came second in a Dolly Parton competition. These are funny stories and I'll remember them. I'll certainly tell them to friends. I've no idea what else I'll do with them, but I might use them in a talk, maybe to illustrate the danger of taking things for granted, or that people don't always prefer the original version.

Stories that
happened to me

Stories that happened
to someone I know

Stories I read
or hear about

Fig 3.12

Watch other presenters and store away ideas from them.   I don't go around thinking I need another story for my storytelling seminar. It's the other way round: Things happen and I think, "Maybe I could use that story to illustrate a point."'

A prop or demonstration

This is one of the most neglected storytelling techniques. It's a bit like 'show and tell' at school. Show people something and how it works and you'll immediately elevate yourself above most presenters and presentations they ever see. TED talks are a great source of inspiration for presenters. A number of the speakers use props and demonstrations to make their point. Here are some of my favourites:

Bill Gates gave a great TED talk about malaria. He came onto the stage with a jar and told the audience, *"There's more money spent on baldness drugs than on malaria. Now baldness is a terrible thing (audience laughs) and rich men are afflicted... that's why that priority's been set. But malaria kills about a million people a year, and 200 million people are suffering from it at any one time.*

Now malaria is of course transmitted by mosquitoes. I brought some here. I'll just take the lid off and let them roam around the auditorium so you can experience them. [He took off the lid, and shook the jar so the mosquitoes flew out.] *There's no reason why only poor people should have the experience!"* People were ducking and diving to avoid the flying insects. Gates let this go on for two or three seconds and then said, *"Don't worry. Those mosquitoes aren't infected...you're under no threat. But now I have your attention...."* The episode made it into the news media all over the world, with headlines about the world's richest man unleashing a swarm of mosquitoes on an unsuspecting audience. Of course, it triggered a huge upsurge in awareness of his cause: a malaria vaccine. You can see the clip here:

https://www.youtube.com/watch?v=ppDWD3VwxVg

Environmentalist Jane Goodall made great use of props in her powerful TED talk 'What separates us from chimpanzees?' She had her monkey doll sitting on the lectern, and produced a piece of Nelson Mandela's Robben Island prison wall to make a point about the importance of hope. But even more memorable were her 'sound props,' when she noisily replicated a chimpanzee greeting from the forests of Tanzania. Her final prop was both solid and sound. She ended her talk with a bell made from a defused landmine from the killing fields of Cambodia. She told the story, rang the bell, and the audience fell silent. Storytelling of the highest order!

https://www.ted.com/talks/jane_goodall_on_what_separates_us_from_the_apes

Engineer Michael Pritchard used a prop to great effect in another TED talk. He invented 'The Lifesaver,' a water filtration device which can turn dirty water into clean drinking water. If adopted worldwide, this would save millions of lives a year. His style was dynamic and his talk was inspiring on its own. However, it reached a new level when he demonstrated the device on stage. People were astounded at its efficacy. Pritchard estimated that by using the LifeSaver bottle, reaching the millennium goal of halving the number of people without drinking water would cost $8 billion, and that $20 billion would provide drinking water for everyone on earth. You can see his talk and demonstration here:

https://www.ted.com/talks/michael_pritchard_invents_a_water_filter

John Kotter and Dan Cohen tell a great story about using props in their book 'The Heart of Change.' It concerns a senior employee in an international company who was convinced his employers were wasting millions of dollars by having lax purchasing policies. This meant they were buying the same items from many different suppliers and paying vastly different costs for them. He set a summer intern the task of investigating the purchases of just one item – work gloves, which all the workers wore. The intern discovered the company was purchasing 424 different types of gloves! The price variation was huge – what cost $5 at one factory was $17 at another.

He ordered one of every type, and he and the intern put price labels on them. He then piled up all the gloves on the board room table and called a meeting of the directors. The directors came in and were astonished at what they saw. Then they walked round the table looking at the price tags. They saw, for example, that two identical gloves were priced $3.22 and $10.55. They agreed this was crazy and changed the purchasing policies.

I've seen many effective uses of props in the medical and scientific world. For example, I once saw an eminent surgeon inflate a surgical glove and stick a pin in different parts of it (fingers and palm). He used it to illustrate the difference between pressure and surface tension, and why he was able to operate on a particular part of the heart with very little risk.

The power of images

The human brain processes images faster than speech and text, and people remember pictures longer than words...but if you can use both together, you're onto a winner.   Think of recent TV news footage. What stands out in your mind?   If we think of the tornados, the floods and hurricanes in the US we mentally see the people stuck on buildings being rescued, old people in dinghies going down what used to be roads. If we think of the migration crisis, we think of migrants being rescued from boats, the little boy dead on the beach and the father finding his missing child. When we recall earthquakes, we see people being rescued after being buried alive for days. These and many other examples convey the power of an image.

Nikki Haley, The US Ambassador to the United Nations, made an impassioned speech to the UN Security Council after a chemical attack launched by the Assad regime targeted children. She stood up and showed photographs of the children who had been horrifically wounded in the attack:

Her words conveyed the raw emotion she felt:

"I will say in the life of the United Nations, there are times when we are compelled to do more than just talk. There are times we are compelled to take collective action. This Security Council thinks of itself as a defender of peace, security, and human rights. We will not deserve that description if we do not rise to action today.

Yesterday morning, we awoke to pictures, to children foaming at the mouth, suffering convulsions, being carried in the arms of desperate parents. We saw rows of lifeless bodies. Some still in diapers. Some with the visible scars of a chemical weapons attack.

Look at those pictures. We cannot close our eyes to those pictures. We cannot close our minds of the responsibility to act. We don't yet know everything about yesterday's attack. But there are many things we do know."

Note that the first two paragraphs are based on *ethos,* drawing on the role, reputation and experience of the United Nations. The other two paragraphs I quoted here (the speech itself was longer and is available online) are pure *pathos.*

However, powerful images are not confined to the fields of tragedy and human suffering. They work at the other end of the scale, for example, with children who meet their heroes, Olympic medal winners or great human interest stories.

In my medical presentations I often use a photograph of a virus or bacteria, an x-ray or scan to illustrate the point I want to make. I sometimes use an electron microscope image of the hepatitis C virus, and say, "Every story has a hero, a victim and a villain. This is the villain. The victims are people with hepatitis. And you are the hero - because you've rescued the victims." One of the most powerful videos I ever saw was of a patient with Parkinson's Disease who had been treated with an experimental drug. His progress was recorded on video over the course of a few months. The difference in his walking and motor function was just extraordinary. It brought home to the audience the potential of this new drug in a way that curves, graphs, charts and data never could.

Paint a picture

'The tongue can paint what the eye can't see' is apparently a Chinese proverb. It encourages us to paint mental pictures. The best presenters (and authors) use imagery in imaginative and interesting ways. They paint pictures with their words:

'We shall defend our island, whatever the cost may be. We shall fight on the beaches, we shall fight on the landing grounds, we shall fight in the fields and in the streets, we shall fight in the hills; we shall never surrender.'

(Winston Churchill)

"Now is the time to rise from the dark and desolate valley of segregation to the sunlit path of racial justice. [...] I have a dream that one day on the red hills of Georgia, the sons of former slaves and the sons of former slave owners will be able to sit down together at the table of brotherhood.'

(Martin Luther King)

"I see Americans of every party, every background, every faith who believe that we are stronger together: black, white, Latino, Asian, Native American; young, old; gay, straight; men, women, folks with disabilities, all pledging allegiance under the same proud flag to this big, bold country that we love. That's what I see. That's the America I know!'

(Barack Obama)

Marie Colvin was a legendary war correspondent who worked for the Sunday Times, London. She had lost her sight in one eye following a grenade attack in Sri Lanka in 2001. In 2010, she gave a speech at a memorial service honouring journalists who had sacrificed their lives.. She painted a graphic word picture in her speech:

"Despite all the videos you see from the Ministry of Defence or the Pentagon, and all the sanitised language describing smart bombs and pinpoint strikes, the scene on the ground has remained remarkably the same for hundreds of years. Craters. Burned houses. Mutilated bodies. Women weeping for children and husbands. Men for their wives, mothers for their children."

Two years later, she was murdered after crossing into Syria on the back of a motor bike to report on the civil war.

The radio is a great place to find examples of word pictures. Wendy Mitchell is a British woman, diagnosed with Alzheimer's Disease at age 58, who wrote a very moving book about how it felt as the terrible disease took hold of her brain. The book, 'Somebody I used to know' was serialised on the BBC. In one of the most memorable passages she describes how she explained the diagnosis and the disease to her workmates:

"I told them the brain is like a bookcase which gets filled up from the bottom, so the most recent memories are at the top, and my oldest ones down near the floor. Now imagine an earthquake comes, and shakes the bookcase vigorously. The books at the top - the recent memories - will all fall out, but those at the bottom will stay put. That's what happens with Alzheimer's. Which explains why I can remember who was in my class at school but have no idea what I had for dinner last night."

I think that's brilliantly inspirational, and hope you do, too. Shakespeare also knew the power of word pictures:

"Once more unto the breach, dear friends, once more;

Or close the wall up with our English dead.

In peace there's nothing so becomes a man

As modest stillness and humility:

But when the blast of war blows in our ears,

Then imitate the action of the tiger;

Stiffen the sinews, summon up the blood,

Disguise fair nature with hard-favour'd rage."

William Shakespeare
Henry V

Whenever we tell a story we paint a picture with words. You may be relating a humorous or startling incident to your friends, describing an incident at work, or telling them about a great sporting event or concert. The ability to do this is one of the attributes of a great storyteller. In fact, you could say if you cannot paint a word picture you cannot tell stories. I use word pictures in my presentations regularly, and I urge you to do the same. I also see some great examples from other presenters. Recently I was working with diabetes specialists and asked them to come up with a word picture to grab the audience's attention. One of them said, *"As you probably know, untreated diabetes is the biggest cause of preventable blindness. I've been working in diabetes for nearly 30 years. The biggest difference I've seen during that time is that I never see dogs in the waiting room. When I was a young physician, there were always one or two guide dogs, helping people with diabetes who had lost their sight. We don't see that anymore...that's a great sign of how much better we have become at treating this terrible condition."*

Turn off the projector and talk to the people! Here's another example from my own experience:

I was in Geneva, Switzerland, moderating a panel discussion on infectious diseases at the time of the Ebola crisis in Sierra Leone. As we came to this part of the programme I said to the audience:

"Now we're moving on to Ebola. Before we do that I'd like to paint a picture of what is happening there today while we're sitting here in our warm, comfortable conference centre. In Sierra Leone there's nowhere left to bury the dead. So when a person dies, of anything, but primarily it is Ebola at the moment, the family wrap the body in a sheet and hire a local fisherman to row the deceased to a neighbouring Island for burial. In reality the fisherman doesn't bury the body in the sense you or I would understand it. They make a shallow indentation in the

ground and put the body in next to the previous night's body and cover it with a little earth. They then wipe their hands on their clothes and go out fishing. They handle the fish and sell them in the market to the people who are already at risk of Ebola.

The question is: 'What can the World Health Organisation do to interrupt that route of transmission of the virus? We are fortunate that on our panel today we have somebody from the WHO who can answer that question. He is Professor X Y Z and I'm delighted to ask him to open the panel discussion. Professor, what are you doing to alleviate the situation in Sierra Leone?"

There are two other points to make about that story. One, I had told the professor what I was going to say. This was because I wanted to check my facts, and I didn't want to catch him out with my emotive picture. The other point is that I personalised the story slightly. I did this by using the phrase: 'while we're sitting here in our warm conference centre.' This encouraged the audience to think about the contrast between Sierra Leone and the conference Hall in Geneva.

Exercise 6

Think about your own presentations, or your own work, and come up with some ideas where you could use memorable moments to tell powerful stories. Think of your favourite stories and see if you can find a genuine use for them to illustrate a point.

And...But...Therefore

Now I want to turn to my final storytelling technique. First, I want to tell you what fails. Here is how NOT to engage and inspire an audience in a presentation:

And..and...and...

Next line, next slide, next line...

And...and..and..and....

.............z z z.

This is what we call the **And...And...And...**way of communicating, or **AAA.** It's boring and dull. It's a classic case of all information, no engagement or inspiration. If you're going to do that, you might as well give the audience a book or an article to read.

However a solution is at hand. You just need to change AAA to ABT. Change And...And...And to

And...But...Therefore....

The difference is stark. There's something happening with **And...But...Therefore...** which doesn't happen with And...And... And.... I think of AAA as a pile of unconnected facts piled up on the floor. ABT assembles them into a story.

With **And...But...Therefore...** there's movement and narrative. Something's happening. It sets up a current situation, introduces a problem, and arrives at a potential solution.

The great screenwriter, Aaron Sorkin, talks about the essence

142

of drama, whether on film, on stage or in a novel, as being 'intention and obstacle.' He says the intention has to be great and the obstacle appear insurmountable. The audience then enjoys watching the hero try to overcome the obstacle to meet his or her goal. The ABT technique is based on the same idea. It's no surprise therefore that Hollywood movies and great TV programmes and books are all based on the same thing. I invite you to take this technique and adopt it into your presenting and storytelling. Here are some examples which I use in my storytelling seminars. I've taken online plot summaries of famous movies and applied the ABT technique to them.

The Wizard of Oz

*There's a little girl living on a farm in Kansas **and** her life is boring **but** one day a a tornado sweeps her away to the land of Oz. **Therefore** she must undertake a difficult and dangerous journey to find her way home.*

Star Wars

The opening caption for the first Star Wars movie reads as follows:

*It is a period of civil war. **And** rebel spaceships striking from a hidden base have won their first victory against the evil Galactic Empire. **But** during the battle rebel spies have managed to steal secret plans to The Empire's ultimate weapon the death star and how much space station with enough power to destroy an entire planet. **Therefore** pursued by The Empire's Sinister agents Princess Leia races home aboard the starship, custodian of the stolen plans that can save her people and restore freedom to the Galaxy.*

Politics also benefits from the ABT technique. You will see it in some of the speeches I've quoted so far from JFK and Martin Luther King. Here's another great example where I've applied the ABC technique: Abraham Lincoln's Gettysburg Address:

*"Four score and seven years ago, our fathers brought forth on this continent, a new nation, conceived in Liberty, **and** dedicated to the proposition that all men are created equal.*

[But] Now we are engaged in a great civil war, testing whether that nation, or any nation so conceived and so dedicated, can long endure. We are met on a great battle-field of that war. We have come to dedicate a portion of that field, as a final resting place for those who here gave their lives that that nation might live. It is altogether fitting and proper that we should do this.

[Therefore] But, in a larger sense, we cannot dedicate -- we cannot consecrate -- we cannot hallow -- this ground. The brave men, living and dead, who struggled here, have consecrated it, far above our poor power to add or detract. The world will little note, nor long remember what we say here, but it can never forget what they did here. It is for us the living, rather, to be dedicated here to the unfinished work which they who fought here have thus far so nobly advanced. It is rather for us to be here dedicated to the great task remaining before us -- that from these honored dead we take increased devotion to that cause for which they gave the last full measure of devotion -- that we here highly resolve that these dead shall not have died in vain -- that this nation, under God, shall have a new birth of freedom -- and that government of the people, by the people, for the people, shall not perish from the earth."

Many of the best medical and scientific papers are also based on the **and...but...therefore..** technique. The discovery of the human genome by British scientists Watson and Crick was, in the opinion of many, the greatest biological scientific achievement of the 20th century. Here's their original paper, published in *Nature* in 1953:

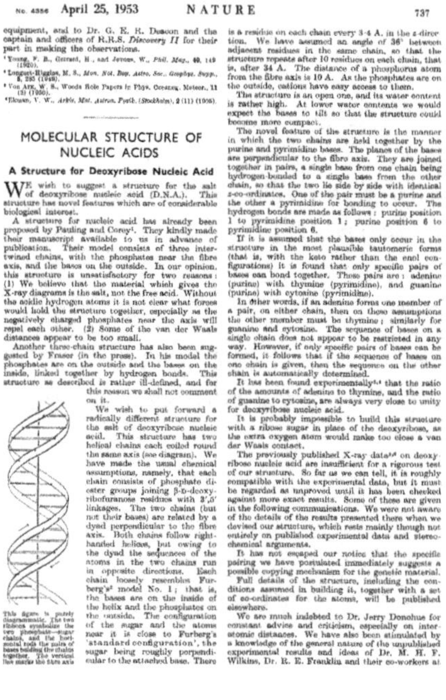

No. 4356 April 25, 1953 NATURE 737

equipment, and to Dr. G. E. R. Deacon and the captain and officers of R.R.S. *Discovery II* for their part in making the observations.

[1] Young, F. B., Gerrard, H., and Jevons, W., *Phil. Mag.*, 40, 149 (1920).
[2] Longuet-Higgins, M. S., *Mon. Not. Roy. Astro. Soc., Geophys. Supp.*, 5, 285 (1949).
[3] Von Arx, W. S., Woods Hole Papers in Phys. Oceanog. Meteor., 11 (3) (1950).
[4] Ekman, V. W., *Arkiv. Mat. Astron. Fysik.* (Stockholm), 2 (11) (1905).

MOLECULAR STRUCTURE OF NUCLEIC ACIDS

A Structure for Deoxyribose Nucleic Acid

WE wish to suggest a structure for the salt of deoxyribose nucleic acid (D.N.A.). This structure has novel features which are of considerable biological interest.

A structure for nucleic acid has already been proposed by Pauling and Corey[1]. They kindly made their manuscript available to us in advance of publication. Their model consists of three intertwined chains, with the phosphates near the fibre axis, and the bases on the outside. In our opinion, this structure is unsatisfactory for two reasons: (1) We believe that the material which gives the X-ray diagrams is the salt, not the free acid. Without the acidic hydrogen atoms it is not clear what forces would hold the structure together, especially as the negatively charged phosphates near the axis will repel each other. (2) Some of the van der Waals distances appear to be too small.

Another three-chain structure has also been suggested by Fraser (in the press). In his model the phosphates are on the outside and the bases on the inside, linked together by hydrogen bonds. This structure as described is rather ill-defined, and for this reason we shall not comment on it.

We wish to put forward a radically different structure for the salt of deoxyribose nucleic acid. This structure has two helical chains each coiled round the same axis (see diagram). We have made the usual chemical assumptions, namely, that each chain consists of phosphate di-ester groups joining β-D-deoxy-ribofuranose residues with 3',5' linkages. The two chains (but not their bases) are related by a dyad perpendicular to the fibre axis. Both chains follow right-handed helices, but owing to the dyad the sequences of the atoms in the two chains run in opposite directions. Each chain loosely resembles Furberg's[2] model No. 1; that is, the bases are on the inside of the helix and the phosphates on the outside. The configuration of the sugar and the atoms near it is close to Furberg's 'standard configuration', the sugar being roughly perpendicular to the attached base. There is a residue on each chain every 3·4 A. in the z-direction. We have assumed an angle of 36° between adjacent residues in the same chain, so that the structure repeats after 10 residues on each chain, that is, after 34 A. The distance of a phosphorus atom from the fibre axis is 10 A. As the phosphates are on the outside, cations have easy access to them.

This figure is purely diagrammatic. The two ribbons symbolize the two phosphate—sugar chains, and the horizontal rods the pairs of bases holding the chains together. The vertical line marks the fibre axis

The structure is an open one, and its water content is rather high. At lower water contents we would expect the bases to tilt so that the structure could become more compact.

The novel feature of the structure is the manner in which the two chains are held together by the purine and pyrimidine bases. The planes of the bases are perpendicular to the fibre axis. They are joined together in pairs, a single base from one chain being hydrogen-bonded to a single base from the other chain, so that the two lie side by side with identical z-co-ordinates. One of the pair must be a purine and the other a pyrimidine for bonding to occur. The hydrogen bonds are made as follows: purine position 1 to pyrimidine position 1; purine position 6 to pyrimidine position 6.

If it is assumed that the bases only occur in the structure in the most plausible tautomeric forms (that is, with the keto rather than the enol configurations) it is found that only specific pairs of bases can bond together. These pairs are: adenine (purine) with thymine (pyrimidine), and guanine (purine) with cytosine (pyrimidine).

In other words, if an adenine forms one member of a pair, on either chain, then on these assumptions the other member must be thymine; similarly for guanine and cytosine. The sequence of bases on a single chain does not appear to be restricted in any way. However, if only specific pairs of bases can be formed, it follows that if the sequence of bases on one chain is given, then the sequence on the other chain is automatically determined.

It has been found experimentally[3,4] that the ratio of the amounts of adenine to thymine, and the ratio of guanine to cytosine, are always very close to unity for deoxyribose nucleic acid.

It is probably impossible to build this structure with a ribose sugar in place of the deoxyribose, as the extra oxygen atom would make too close a van der Waals contact.

The previously published X-ray data[5,6] on deoxyribose nucleic acid are insufficient for a rigorous test of our structure. So far as we can tell, it is roughly compatible with the experimental data, but it must be regarded as unproved until it has been checked against more exact results. Some of these are given in the following communications. We were not aware of the details of the results presented there when we devised our structure, which rests mainly though not entirely on published experimental data and stereochemical arguments.

It has not escaped our notice that the specific pairing we have postulated immediately suggests a possible copying mechanism for the genetic material.

Full details of the structure, including the conditions assumed in building it, together with a set of co-ordinates for the atoms, will be published elsewhere.

We are much indebted to Dr. Jerry Donohue for constant advice and criticism, especially on inter-atomic distances. We have also been stimulated by a knowledge of the general nature of the unpublished experimental results and ideas of Dr. M. H. F. Wilkins, Dr. R. E. Franklin and their co-workers at

Fig 3.13

It's based on the ABT technique. Here's the introductory text:

"We wish to suggest a structure for the salt of deoxyribose nucleic acid (D.N.A.). This structure has novel features which are of considerable biological interest. ***[And]*** *A structure for nucleic acid has already been proposed by Pauling and Corey. They kindly made their manuscript available to us in advance of publication. Their model consists of three intertwined chains, with the phosphates near the fibre axis, and the bases on the outside.*

[But] *In our opinion. this structure is unsatisfactory for two reasons: (1) We believe that the material which gives*

the X-ray diagrams is the salt, not the free acid. Without the acidic hydrogen atoms it is not clear what forces would hold the structure together, especially as the negatively charged phosphates near the axis will repel each other. (2) Some of the van der Waals distances appear to be too small. Another three-chain structure has also been suggested by Fraser (in the press). In his model the phosphates are on the outside and the bases on the inside, linked together by hydrogen bonds. This structure as described is rather ill-defined, and for this reason we shall not comment on it.

[Therefore] *We wish to put forward a radically different structure for the salt of deoxyribose nucleic acid. [...]"*

Modern examples are very common, in science and elsewhere:

ABT in action

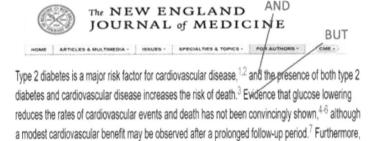

Fig 3.14

Many of the stories I've told in this book can be retold on the

ABT model:

Everyone agrees that electric cars would be environmentally beneficial, **[AND]** the major car manufacturers are spending vast amounts of money developing them. **[BUT]** the main problem is that battery power is still quite limited. **[THEREFORE]** much of the research funding is going into extending the life and reducing the charging time of the batteries.

My father suffered from paranoid schizophrenia **[AND]** his symptoms were treated successfully with medication. **[BUT]** the medication made his hands tremble. This was really problematic for him, as he was a keen artist. **[THEREFORE]** we need drugs that are as effective as that one, but without the side effects.

Alternatives to ABT

It is important to note that 'And...But...Therefore...' is a concept rather than an instruction to use those particular words. Here's a list of alternative words which will enable you to grasp the ABT idea.

And	But	Therefore
also	despite	so
in addition	yet	consequently
equally	however	thus
uniquely	conversely	hence
moreover	whereas	accordingly
as well as	although	as a result

Exercise 7

Think about your own work, projects or presentation. Think about the initial problem you set out to solve. What was the limitation of the current product or service? Think about the unmet need or the gap in the market. What was it that people wanted to do that they couldn't do. What was stopping them? Think about your idea of a solution. Turn these ideas into a brief narrative based on **And...But... Therefore.**

Part 2: summary

- Stories engage the brain more effectively than lists of facts

- Storytelling is not new. It is based on the techniques of rhetoric, which was used by the Ancient Greeks and Romans over 3,000 years ago.

- Aristotle, regarded as the father of rhetoric, said there were three modes of persuasion: *Ethos:* Your standing and reputation, based on your experience learning, expertise and qualifications

- *Logos:* An appeal to logic or reason, using a scientific approach

- *Pathos:* An appeal to emotions, using empathy or evoking sympathy

- Aim to demonstrate maximum *ethos* in every situation, coupled with an appropriate amount of *logos* and *pathos*

- Aim to inform, engage and inspire your audiences. Too many presenters just aim to inform

- Storytelling targets are the head, heart and gut

- Use the 'And, But, Therefore...' technique to tell stories

- Create and use memorable moments in your talks. These include surprising statistics, personal stories, props, great quotes, memorable images and word pictures.

- Use contrast, repetition and questions.

- Make your talks personal to yourself, and to the audience.

PART 3

ARE YOU MISSING THE POINT OF **PowerPoint**?

PowerPoint celebrated its 30th birthday in 2017. Has its existence made you a better or worse presenter? For many presenters, the answer is 'definitely worse'. That's because they've come to rely on it like a child learning to ride a bike relies on the stabilisers. They lean on it and it's reassuring. They use it all the time even when they don't need it, and to be fair to them, part of the time it's useful. It's an accepted way to illustrate talks, and they've always done it in this way. However, many things used to be acceptable that aren't any longer...drunken driving, smoking on aeroplanes, sexist, racist or homophobic behaviour, lead in petrol, asbestos in houses and many more. Maybe it's time you took a look at how you use PowerPoint?

Many people blame PowerPoint for bad presentations

The problem is not the software – it's the way they use it. They're missing the point of PowerPoint. Others wear their anti-PowerPoint credentials like a badge of pride. Some people have even banned it – or claim to. Recently, I was taking a brief from a client who proudly remarked, "I never use PowerPoint in my presentations. I've banned it." She then used PowerPoint to brief me and a colleague about a new project! She didn't regard a meeting for three of us as 'a presentation'. A group of academics who formed an anti-PowerPoint party, entered the Swiss elections and received 4,359 votes! However, with great respect to my client and the academics, I disagree that the world's most-vilified software programme is a force for evil.

PowerPoint is innocent

PowerPoint is an excellent software package for designing slides which, should at least, help your audience understand your talk. It may even do more than that. If you use it really cleverly, it might also help you to be memorable, and help towards engaging and inspiring them.

Notice the key word there: *help*. It can *help* you be clearer, *help* the audience understand, *help* you be memorable. It can't do it alone. Because PowerPoint is a *visual aid*. It's not the point of your talk. It's not leading you, it's supporting you.

Blaming your slides for boring presentations is like blaming cars for road accidents

You're behind the wheel, and are responsible for what happens on the journey. If you substitute *'podium'* for *wheel* in that sentence, you have the truth about your presentation.

As an example, look at Steve Jobs. He was universally acknowledged as a brilliant presenter. PowerPoint didn't ever hold him back as he used it as a tool and made it work for him. You can do that, too, and I want to help you. First, I want you to think differently about your slides. Remember that they're not actually *slides* at all.

The idea of *slides* takes us back to the days when they were literally that...35mm slides, loaded into a carousel which was inserted into a projector.

Kodak invented it, and the projector itself was the centre of an early episode of the *'Mad Men'* TV series. The episode contained a brilliant example of features vs benefits. Don Draper is pitching an idea for a new slide projector to two Kodak executives. He uses it to show a sequence of emotive slides, including him embracing his wife on their wedding day, the birth of a child, a Christmas party and them sitting on the sofa at home. 'This device is a time machine. It takes us backwards, forwards, backwards, forwards in time, to a place where we ache to go back to. Eventually it returns us to the place we call home. It's called the carousel.'

About the only place you'll now find a slide projector is in a museum. Even Amazon and eBay can only offer you used ones. Glass, or plastic, 35mm slides have gone exactly the same way, replaced by pixels and computer code. Unfortunately, our way of thinking has not evolved to the same extent, so we still expect our projected displays to look like *slides*. That's why there are so many bullet points and complicated graphs projected. I want you to think about them differently. Instead of thinking of a deck of slides, think of a *storyboard*.

This involves visually mapping out your story in a sequence of small frames. It's used in TV, film and video production to give an overview of the story.

Presentation types

The main difference between a storyboard and 'The Grid' introduced in part 1 is that the storyboard is visual, whereas The Grid is, generally, text-based. As an introduction to using slides (for the sake of simplicity I will still call them that) you first need to think about what kind of presentation you're planning. Broadly speaking, presentations or talks fall into a number of categories, based on your objective. Examples are:

Informational	Persuasive
Educational	Entertaining
Instructional	Demonstration
Inspirational	Decision time

Some of these overlap. In Steve Jobs' presentations at Macworld, for example, he would introduce a new iProduct (informational), show us how to use it (demonstrational) but also inspire us to go out and buy/sell/use it (inspirational). The category of your talk will influence the type of slides you're going to produce. However, surprise is a key element in making presentations memorable, so don't be put off using, for example, vivid imagery in an otherwise formal setting.

In my own world, I regularly deal with presentations about clinical trials on medical drugs and devices, or corporate presentations about business strategy or finance. They have a heavy bias towards the informational category. However, the point of developing new medicines is to help patients, so there's often a place for patient pictures, used *appropriately* (that word again!). In these talks, the opportunity to use images will be more limited than in other situations - but your slides should still look good!

Slides are *visual aids*. That means, they're supposed to be *visually attractive*, and should be an *aid* to the audience in helping them to understand your talk. Both of these things are important.

Slide categories

Once you've decided what kind of presentation you're going to give, your next step is to consider the type of slides to use. The slides themselves divide broadly into three categories:

- Image-based (Pictorial)

- Graphic- based (Graphical)

- Text-based (Textual)

You then need to think about the purpose of each individual slide. What do you want the slide to do? Here are some answers:

Inform	Demonstrate
Summarise	Explain
Inspire	Illustrate
Provoke	Make people laugh
Be a pretty picture	Create a mood

In any presentation you may have a number of these. What you do need, however, is an overall look for your slides, in terms of fonts, colours and flow.

Pictorial slides

This is the modern way of using slides. Great pictures, strong graphics, big numbers, quotes, thoughtful use of colours. These digital projections are the nearest thing we have to the beautifully designed 35mm slides we had back in the days when they were produced by designers and projected in a darkened hall or lecture theatre. They look great, and when done well, they are extremely effective. The challenge is that, while anyone can type a few bullet points onto a slide, not everyone can produce a beautiful graphic design. This means you may need to get someone else to do it for you, sometimes at extra cost.

However, the cost need not be particularly high. For example, I had these two cartoons drawn and delivered electronically within four hours for just 25 USD. As I've used them countless times since, I regard them to be a good investment. They work well to illustrate the points I want to make, and are unique to me, rather than using common Clip Art that people have seen many times. You can get your entire slide set designed quite cheaply online, and if your company doesn't insist on a rigid template, it's worth considering. Once you have the range of templates, you can add your own numbers and charts.

Figs 3.4 and 3.5

Image-based slides are used in a number of ways. They are sometimes presented as a backdrop to cue a particular mood in the audience while the presenter talks about something appropriate. For example, you may use a picture of a beautiful sunset or a mountain range. The message is: Chill out, relax, life is good.

You can develop this theme by using a sequence of *allegorical* images. For example, you might use a beautiful scene, with blue skies over a calm sea, with a boat sailing thorough it, to create an atmosphere of tranquillity while you talk about the good days of the company. Your next slide might be a stormy sea

159

to illustrate tough times. Your third image could be the crew working hard to keep the boat on course, followed by a huge wave flooding the deck. Slides five and six could be the boat heading for the rocks, and finally a shipwreck, with the crew in lifeboats. In this case, the changing sea is used as an allegory for the changing market conditions, and the ship is the company.

You would have storyboarded this sequence something like this:

Fig 3.6

Another technique in this type of slide-making is to add text to a background picture. You have to be careful here, because balancing visual backgrounds with text is difficult, and needs a creative eye. Very often, the text gets lost in the image. However, with a little creativity, you can overcome this. For example, you might blur or dull the image, or put a coloured wash over it, just as you add the text. Whatever you do, make sure the text stands out and walk to the back of the room to check it from there.

Personally, I think some of these slides miss the mark, because the image can distract from the message if it is inappropriate. Quotes from JFK and Steve Jobs, with backgrounds of sunrise or mountain ranges don't always work. When I use those quotes, I usually use a photograph of them making the speech. There is no doubt that this has relevance and helps to anchor it in the period. However, if you are going to quote the Dalai Lama, pictures of beautiful Tibetan mountain ranges might be entirely appropriate.

A clever way to use an image is to use it to engage the audience by posing a question with it. For example, there has been criticism of pharmaceutical companies and universities for not publishing all the data from some clinical trials. (There are perfectly valid reasons for that, but this is not the place to elaborate). After much debate, it was decided that more data could be published, and the UK and European trade associations would lead the initiative.

I attended a presentation on the subject by Andrew Powrie-Smith, the Director of Communications at the European trade body, EFPIA. He's a great presenter and uses slides very cleverly. His first slide was a photograph of a bubble car:

Fig 3.7

Bubble cars were popular in the 1950s and 60s. They were small, slow, cheap to run, easy to park and a much-loved example of British eccentricity. They're now an iconic symbol of creativity and wackiness in a simpler age.

Andy projects picture of the bubble car and some people smile. (Generally, those old enough to recognise it.) He explains what it is, 'for the benefit of the young people here,' he says with a smile and then asks a question:

"Apart from it being odd, and kind of cool in a strange way, what was unique about the bubble car?"

'It had no reverse gear!' shouts someone from the audience.

"You're right," replies Andy. "My mate Mike's Mum had one. We used to pick the back of it up and turn it round for her in the drive in front of their house! I actually wanted to get a real bubble car in here to illustrate this fact, but I didn't think the budget would stand it, so we won't be doing that today. The point I want to make is that, just like the bubble car, the data transparency initiative has no reverse gear. Once we go with it, there's no going backwards. So we have to get it right, and we need the backing of everyone involved."

How creative is that? How much more memorable, and engaging for the audience, than just to stand up and say, 'Once we do this, we can't change it.' It worked on a number of levels:

- It was interesting. People like to learn things (even if it's something about the drive mechanism of a now-defunct automobile).

- It was amusing, and made the audience laugh

- It involved the audience

- It was memorable

- The picture and the question and answer, were *appropriate*.

The last point is crucial. I see people using pictures, cartoons and other images where the relevance to the point is tenuous at best. I urge you to avoid this. If not, it devalues your presentation, and can even confuse the audience, particularly if you aren't presenting in their native language. Humour, jokes, irony and wit are often lost in translation, and may become a barrier to understanding.

Where do good images come from? Not Microsoft Clip Art. This hasn't been cool or effective for about 10years. Just as presentation technology has moved on, so have the audience's expectations. Your use of pictures should move on too. There are lots of great images available online. Some of them are completely free, and others are royalty-free, meaning you pay an upfront fee and can continue to use them without any extra payment. You'd be amazed how many people won't pay even a few dollars for an image. If you do, your pictures (and therefore your slides) will look different from anyone else's, and you're on the way to being different and memorable!

Exercise 8

Choose one of your own presentations and redesign it using:

1. The storyboard technique

2. Pictorial or graphical slides where appropriate

Graphical slides

It's not only photographs that can add the visual element to your slides. Well-designed graphics can also do a great job. This is particularly the case when the content of your talk is very dense. Financial results presentations are a case in point. They are, obviously, full of numbers and statistics, all of which are important to the analysts and financial media. Thoughtful use of design can really help to aid understanding. Here's an example, taken from the February 2018 annual results from the telecom giant, Orange.

This is the top part of the press release, announcing the key numbers in factual style:

Press release
Paris, 21 February 2018

2017 earnings

Accelerated growth in revenues and adjusted EBITDA and return to growth in Operating Cash Flow[*]

In millions of euros	2017	2016 comparable basis	2016 historical basis	change comparable basis	change historical basis
Revenues	41,096	40,593	40,918	1.2 %	0.4 %
Adjusted EBITDA	12,819	12,538	12,682	2.2 %	1.1 %
Operating Income	4,917		4,077		20.6 %
Consolidated net income of continuing operations	2,114		1,010		
CAPEX (excluding licences)	7,209	6,974	6,971	3.4 %	3.4 %
Operating Cash Flow	5,610	5,564	5,711	0.8 %	(1.8)%

Orange's revenues and adjusted EBITDA grew for the second consecutive year in 2017, while Operating Cash Flow grew for the first time since 2009[*].
- In France, revenue grew for the first time since 2009, up 0.6%;
- In Spain, record growth rates achieved, with revenues up 7.1% and adjusted EBITDA up 17.0%[*];
- In Africa & the Middle East, revenue growth accelerated to 3.0%[*].

Fig 3.8

That's a factual document containing the key information. (There was more of it in the complete press release). Anyone receiving it can read and re-read it, enlarge it on their screens or mark up the printed copy. It works well. However, you wouldn't want to try and present it on a slide using this design. Being clever, thoughtful and creative people at Orange, they know this. So here's a selection of the slides, presented by the Chairman/CEO and CFO, containing the same information:

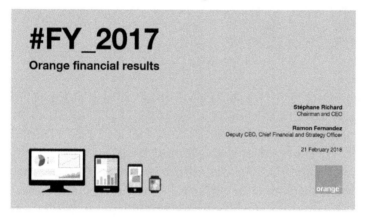

Fig 3.9

This is a model of a clever introduction slide. It's clear, well-designed and gives us crucial information. The #FY_2017 leads to the Twitter feed of the results, with commentary from the Chairman and CEO, among others.

Fig 3.10

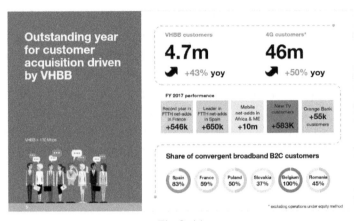

Fig 3.11

Of course, given the subject matter and the legal reporting requirements, there's inevitably a lot of information on these slides. However, remember that these did not stand alone – they were presented and explained at the time by the senior executives. They're an excellent example of how to convey complicated information clearly. The Twitter slides were also redrawn, in an even simpler way, for the social media audience, and the feed included commentary from the Chairman/CEO:

Fig 3.12

One point about graphics: As with images, it's easy to be carried away with the artistic merit. The question you should constantly ask yourself is not 'is this a good graphic?' but 'will this aid understanding?'

As with all presentations, the overall look of the slides must be consistent. It's important that each slide feels like part of a story. To do this, you need to use the same fonts, colours, backgrounds and style of imagery throughout. This will help the audience understand your talk.

Textual slides

When we think of long, dull PowerPoint-led presentations, we normally imagine text-based slides. All too often, they're either composed of long lists of words or bullet points, or crammed with so much text they're unreadable. The font makes the slide look like the bottom line of an eye test chart, and just for good measure, the text colour blends into the background, so it's almost unreadable. This section is not a defence of those techniques...they are tedious, and one of the key reasons for PowerPoint's bad reputation. However, the fact remains that there are times when only text will do. For example:

- When you need to convey specific, accurate information and/or rules

- When you need to show a legal definition and explain what it means to the audience, eg with Healthcare Compliance or Code rules in the pharmaceutical industry

- When you need to ensure the audience clearly understands what will happen next, for example when announcing redundancies or other major changes

- When you need to ensure people know where to go for more information on the topic you've presented.

So let's look at how to produce and successfully use textual slides in a way that aids clear communication for you, and understanding for the audience. Let's start with what slides are NOT:

- **They are not a teleprompter**

- **They are not speaker notes**

- **They are not a script for your talk.**

One of the seven challenges of communicating science I outlined earlier was, 'It's not about the PowerPoint.'

This advice is not just relevant to scientific presenters, of course – it's relevant to anyone. Too many presenters use PowerPoint, or other presentation software, as a crutch rather than an aid. Other presenters read their slides, often while looking at the screen, using the slides as a teleprompter. In this case, their voice becomes no more than a sound track for the slides.

This approach fails for a number of reasons:

It puts the slides at the centre stage rather than the presenter. If you're going to play the supporting role in this way, you may as well just send the slides. If the words coming out of your mouth are the same as those on your slides, one of those is not necessary. Don't write yourself out of the script!

PowerPoint is designed to be a medium of impression, not information. This means that your slides are not a great means of conveying the details of your work. This is best done in other ways, such as a handout, or a published paper in a peer-reviewed journal. However, if you have clearly divergent Kaplan-Meier curves visually illustrating how people lived longer whilst taking your new drug, a colourful pie chart showing how people access your online product by apps rather than on their laptops, or a bar chart clearly showing how your sales breakdown has changed since you launched a new marketing campaign, PowerPoint is a great way of conveying it.

Many presenters create problems themselves by the way they develop their talk. They start with the slides (which are often produced by someone else trying to be helpful) and work back towards a presentation. This produces the 'talking through some slides' style of presentation I criticised in the previous section. That is putting the cart before the horse. You need to start with the story, clarify what you want to say, and only then add visual aids *where necessary* to help you say it.

Alternatives to slides

Before I turn to the use, misuse and abuse of PowerPoint, I would like you to consider other ways of illustrating your talk. As with so many aspects of presenting, *appropriateness* is the key concept. What is appropriate for ten people in a room, may not work with 500 in a lecture theatre. Here are some ideas:

Flipcharts

In these high-tech days, the humble flipchart seems to have lost out to its flashier cousins. This is unfortunate because, in some circumstances, a flipchart has advantages over other visual aids.

In front of a small group, a flipchart encourages interactivity and generates a sense of energy

This is particularly relevant if you draw on it live, in front of the group. It allows you to take the group with you as you build your story. It can be great for illustrating the flow of patients through a trial, or a timeline of events, such as the key steps in a drug development programme.

Use thick pens and a range of bright colours for best effect. Draw in wide, bold strokes and use all the available space. Don't be afraid to use it with a large audience: hook up a camera to your laptop and project the flipchart image on a large screen.

Earlier, I referred to the talk on Pulse Pressure I saw at a cardiology meeting. The presenter, a Japanese professor, gave a masterful presentation using a flipchart and a thick red pen.

He began with a clear statement: *"I want you to think*

differently about blood pressure. This is how we typically record it...systolic over diastolic. Let's say (here he drew on the flipchart in large numbers) *120 over 80. For your patients over 50 years old, I want you to forget about diastolic pressure. (Here he crossed out the lower number with a flourish). And I want you to think instead about the difference between the two numbers...in this case 40. That is the pulse pressure, and there is increasing evidence that it is a good indicator of heart health. That's what I want to talk about."*

He then used PowerPoint slides very effectively for the rest of his talk, but his flipchart opener did a great job.

The example I quoted of the scientist who talked about the patient benefits of the human genome project is another example of an effective use of a flipchart. (He used a whiteboard, but the technique is the same).

Video

When used appropriately (that word again!) video can be the most powerful element of your presentation. It allows you to mentally transport the audience somewhere else, or bring another person, place or thing into the hall with you. Patient testimonials and case studies often work well on video. Talking to a hall full of doctors and scientists can be intimidating at the best of times for people who aren't used to it, so having a video recording of a patient is safer than expecting them to perform live under such stress.

I once hosted a press conference at an international rheumatology congress where a German patient was one of the speakers. In the rehearsal she was relaxed and told her story well in good English. When we went live, however, her nerves took over, and she answered all my English questions in German! Fortunately, her physician was also on the panel, so he translated.

Some of the most memorable presentations I've seen incorporated dramatic video clips. In one, the presenter was a neurologist who showed a Parkinson's disease patient before and after going on an experimental new treatment. The difference in the amount of control the patient had over his movements was hugely impressive, and the effect of the video was dramatic. It brought the point of developing new medicines into the room in a way nothing else could.

Two tips if you are going to use video:

- Keep the clips short. Like your presentation, they should be 'as short as possible but as long as necessary.' You can always include a link to the longer version, if required.

- Get them edited professionally. Or learn to do it yourself – you can learn very quickly online. People see so much high-quality video today, anything which appears sub-standard can harm not only your presentation, but also your credibility.

Handouts

A bit like the flipchart, handouts are unfashionable but can work well in small groups. They're useful when you want the others in the meeting to go through detailed figures and text. Although you can do this on a slide (in a small group), giving each person their own copy on which they can make notes and comments is a real aid to understanding. If you're going to use handouts, be clear about what you want them to achieve. If they contain additional or supplementary information, remember to give people time to read them. Either send them as a pre-read, or allocate reading time in the session. If they are a printout of your slides, you can usually save the distribution until the end. Tell them that, and encourage them to sit back and enjoy your talk.

A word here about one of the most-neglected elements of

PowerPoint...the 'Notes Pages' view. Many of the problems of dense slides can be solved by including a summary of your commentary on the Notes Pages for a handout, rather than cluttering up your slides.

Props

A prop can be a great way of illustrating something. See the section on *Creating a Memorable Moment* in Part 2 for more ideas and examples.

You!

You're the star of the show, and you can be your best visual aid. Earlier in the book I described cardiologist, Salim Yusuf's, address to more than 100 journalists at 6.30am in Chicago. It's an excellent illustration of the power of the human presence, particularly one as charismatic as Professor Yusuf. If you really want to be radical, you could try not having any other visual aids at all. This would be a brave move, but it would certainly get the audience's attention...your task would be to hold it for the duration of your talk.

You also need to plan for what happens if the AV system breaks down or there's a power outage. This has happened to me occasionally, and I hope I've managed to cope with it well. My most memorable experience was at a conference in Istanbul when suddenly the lights in the auditorium went out. A few seconds later they came back on, as the emergency lighting kicked in. I was on stage, mid-presentation. The emergency lighting did not include the AV system, so I didn't have any slides or microphone. At that moment a man in a high visibility vest appeared at the door with a loud hailer. He addressed us all through it, telling us that everything was fine, and the power would be back on very soon. I asked if I could borrow his loud hailer, but understandably he had other uses for it! So I carried on with a simplified version of my talk, with no slides, from the middle of the room so everyone could hear me. I hope it worked.

In reality, if you're presenting complex information to people who need to understand it. you'll need to illustrate it. In most cases, this will mean using PowerPoint or other presentation software. Obviously this is not the case with chance encounters and ad hoc conversations that take place in coffee queues and around water coolers in conference centres and offices. In these circumstances you'll have no help at all, which is why you need to become fluent at telling the story without any visual aids except yourself.

Before I turn to designing and using PowerPoint slides in detail, I want to clarify two points:

- When I talk about using PowerPoint I mean presentation software of any type.

- For the rest of this chapter I'll discuss how to use slides during a presentation to a group of people. There's nothing wrong with using complicated graphs, tables and similar when discussing the fine details of your research with others who are closely involved. In science and medicine, and in the STEM (Science, Technology, Engineering, Maths) areas in particular, the devil is in the detail and it's crucial that the detail is closely examined before you start to produce your talk. See the story about the effect of PowerPoint on the Challenger disaster for a clear illustration of this.

PowerPoint is innocent!

PowerPoint is one of the most maligned and misunderstood tools available in the computer age.

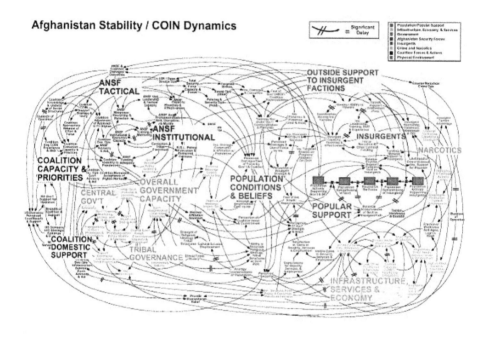

Fig 3.13

The US Army apparently banned PowerPoint in 2011 in military briefings, after the above slide caused confusion and derision in equal measure: US General, Stanley McCrystal, joked *'When we understand it, we'll have won the war.'* He then banned PowerPoint from future briefings. However, the Pentagon even topped that with another monster: This epic was presented, then printed as a wall chart to explain the process for developing, buying, and maintaining gear:

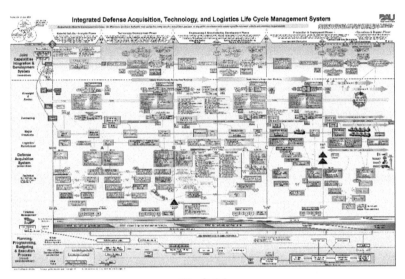

Fig 3.14

I see many complicated slides at medical congresses, and I'm sure you do too in your own area of business. In their own way some are as confusing as this. I will introduce some of them later in this chapter.

Reasons for bad slides

In my view, there are three main reasons for bad or unclear slides:

- Inappropriate usage

- Muddled thinking.

- Too much information

Inappropriate usage

PowerPoint is a very good software package, designed to illustrate presentations. Its aim is to make presentations and talks easier to understand. However, for a number of reasons, it has become the standard way of producing documents which would be better in another form, for example as Microsoft Word, Adobe Acrobat (pdf) or Excel spreadsheets.

Many people in large companies produce PowerPoint 'decks' (to use the American term) as their basic information resource rather than as a presentation aid. They circulate these around the company for comment, and however clear they were at the beginning, the slides become busier and more cluttered. At the end of this process, someone has to try and present these slides as visual aids...which by then, they most definitely are not. Some people in the audience will be thinking, 'Those slides look terrible!' Often, the very people who've had a hand in the process!

The most tragic instance of inappropriate usage of PowerPoint concerned the Columbia Space Shuttle disaster in 2003, when the spacecraft disintegrated over Texas while re-entering the earth's atmosphere. The tragic sequence of events began days earlier, when a small piece of foam insulation broke off on take-off. Engineers urgently attempted to predict whether the missing piece might cause a serious problem on re-entry. They made their report to senior managers, while Columbia was still in space, in a PowerPoint presentation of 28 slides, rather than in a detailed engineering report. As the two inquiry reports stated:

"Many of the engineering packages brought before formal control boards were documented only in PowerPoint presentations. It appears that many young engineers do not understand the need for, or know how to prepare, formal engineering documents such as reports, white papers or analyses."

From the Return to Flight Task Group, set up after the disaster - criticism focused on one complicated slide in particular:

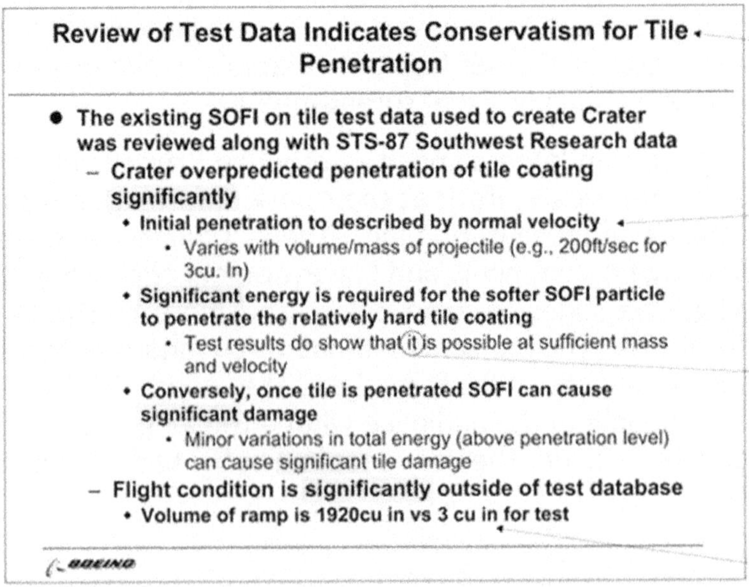

Review of Test Data Indicates Conservatism for Tile Penetration

- ● **The existing SOFI on tile test data used to create Crater was reviewed along with STS-87 Southwest Research data**
  - — **Crater overpredicted penetration of tile coating significantly**
    - • **Initial penetration to described by normal velocity**
      - • Varies with volume/mass of projectile (e.g., 200ft/sec for 3cu. In)
    - • **Significant energy is required for the softer SOFI particle to penetrate the relatively hard tile coating**
      - • Test results do show that it is possible at sufficient mass and velocity
    - • **Conversely, once tile is penetrated SOFI can cause significant damage**
      - • Minor variations in total energy (above penetration level) can cause significant tile damage
  - — **Flight condition is significantly outside of test database**
    - • **Volume of ramp is 1920cu in vs 3 cu in for test**

BOEING

Fig 3.15

The bottom bullet point, translated into understandable language, means the volume of foam which may hit the shuttle was 640 times larger than previously estimated, and therefore posed a significant risk to the vessel. This point was not understood by NASA officials who had to make life or death decisions based on the presentation. As we know, Columbia exploded on re-entry, killing the seven astronauts on board.

Prof Tuffte (quoted earlier) analysed the PowerPoint slides and produced a damning critique. The official accident inquiry was also highly critical.

"As information gets passed up an organization hierarchy, from people who do analysis to mid-level managers to high-level leadership, key explanations and supporting information is filtered out. In this context, it is easy to understand how a senior manager might read this PowerPoint slide and not realize that it addresses a life-threatening situation."

From the report of the Columbia Accident Investigation Board

Muddled thinking

Unclear slides are often an illustration and a consequence of unclear thinking. People produce slides with too much information because they haven't gone through the mental exercise of asking themselves, 'what does the slide need to say here to support my point?' They have often failed to do this with their presentation as a whole, or with the individual slides. As I suggested earlier, you need to plan your talk like a story, with a clear narrative. Only then do you add in the slides. Remember:

Ideas come first

Words come next

Slides come last

Think of your presentation like a jigsaw puzzle where every piece is a slide.
They all have a role to play, and must fit together perfectly

Too much information

Of necessity, data sets include a lot of information. However, that doesn't mean you need to put it all on a slide. It doesn't even mean you need to present it all. A basic, but common error which scientific and medical presenters make is this: They confuse what's appropriate to include in a journal paper with what can be understood when presented on a slide.

Don't confuse the paper with the presentation

When people read a research paper or a detailed report, they can pore over it, examine the detail and go back to earlier sections when necessary to help them understand it. In a presentation, none of this is possible. The audience has to understand it at the first pass, and as the presenter you have a responsibility to facilitate that. It isn't enough to paste in graphics and charts from the paper. At the very least, they should be redrawn so they appear more visually clear.

One problem for scientific data presenters is this:

In a report of a clinical trial, the devil is in the detail

So how much detail should you include? If you are presenting the results of a clinical trial, do you really need to show us the trial design, patient characteristics at baseline, their comorbidities and concomitant medications? The answer is, 'Yes, if this information is needed to enable your audience to make an accurate assessment of the study.' A data presentation is not like many other types of talk. It needs detail, and it needs to be thorough. The challenge is in deciding exactly how much detail to include. Too much and it becomes confusing, interrupts the narrative and leads the story up blind alleys. Too little detail and you may be accused of not being sufficiently rigorous or of concealing important information.

No two trials are the same, and there is no general advice I can give you which will allow you to get the balance right every time. Generally speaking, the patient characteristics are only worth highlighting if there's an important difference between them, and definitely if this could affect the results. If you have more obese patients, or more with diabetes or compromised kidney function in one group than another, you would of course mention it.

However, important differences may only become obvious later, and you need to be adaptable. I was working with a company which had produced a new type of anti-platelet agent which, according to their major trial, was significantly superior to the existing medication. About the time that the results were presented at a major European conference, claims emerged that another type of drug known as a PPI, or a Proton Pump Inhibitor, could interfere with the efficacy of anti-platelet agents. Concomitant PPI used in patients in both arms of the study then became an important factor, and was rightly included in the later presentations, although it had been omitted from the early versions.

On another occasion, the size of the loading dose in the comparator arm in an earlier trial was criticised. This was addressed in the later, larger study, where individual physicians were left to decide which dose to use. When the phase III results were presented, this point was included in the trial design slide, and was highlighted briefly by presenters.

Think of it this way: If a company is listed on the stock exchanges, anything which could be regarded as 'material' to the stock price has to be disclosed. I urge you to take the same attitude to the fine details in your presentation...if they could become 'material,' include them on a slide, and highlight them verbally. Also remember that your slides are not produced to stand alone. When you present them, you have the responsibility to highlight what is important. Your slides must enable this.

Declutter your slides

Having decided how much detail you need to **include,** now look at your slides another way: how much can you fairly **exclude?** Cluttered slides look messy, suggest a lack of intellectual rigour and are confusing to the audience. Declutter your slides and your presentation will soar to new heights of clarity. Strip out anything which isn't essential. Use the jigsaw puzzle analogy I introduced earlier to every element of every slide. Ask yourself whether you really need it on that slide, or in the notes pages, or should it only feature in the paper.

Here are some guidelines for producing decluttered, clear slides:

- Ensure that every slide has a clear message

- Every slide should have a clear title.#

- Title should summarise the content where possible. Eg, *'Statins reduce CV events'* is better than ' *Relationship between statin use and CV events'*.

- Every element on the slide should be necessary and clear

- The whole deck should have a logical flow

- Keep text to a minimum and make it large enough to read from the back

- Use clearly differentiated colours to differentiate key elements

- Use a light background and dark text or vice versa

- Backgrounds and templates should be uncluttered, with only minimal logos and other identifiers

- The design of the slides should be consistent, eg the same colour for the active compound, comparator and placebo throughout the whole set

- Lines and curves should be thick enough to stand out

- Lines and curves should be clearly differentiated by colour

- Charts (especially black and white charts) should not be pasted in from papers and journals

- Scales should be clear

- Spell out unfamiliar abbreviations

- Keep references to a minimum

- Use phrases, not sentences, unless there is a legal reason to do so

- Add arrows or boxes to highlight key points, eg difference on Kaplan-Meier curves

- Avoid excessive numbers of fonts and colours

- Use sans serif fonts eg Verdana, Arial, Helvetica and Tahoma (as approved by the FDA)

- If you have to use a complicated slide, use animation to build it up and take the audience through the logical process. Watch TV news to see how they build up quite complicated graphics quickly, then follow their lead.

For pictorial slides:

- Use visually striking images, strong graphics and

colours

- If adding text to an image, make sure both elements work well together

- Make sure the text is readable and does not get lost in the image.

Examples: Poor slide design

I've used medical and scientific examples in this book because their subject matter is complex, and simplifying it is challenging. The guidelines I'm outlining, however, are relevant to any area and any presenter. This section contains some slides I've seen presented at meetings and congresses, and others which are available online. In some cases I've changed figures and other key details to spare the embarrassment of those involved. In all cases, my comments are aimed at the design of the slides and how much information is on them, rather than the details of the information itself. I don't intend to list every PowerPoint data sin here, but to give a few examples to illustrate common faults and suggest improvements.

CML mutations

Some people develop a type of blood cancer called Chronic Myeloid Leukemia (CML). They are treated with drugs called Tyrosine Kinase Inhibitors (TKIs). The most common one is called imatinib, or Gleevec. However, over time, they develop mutations in their genes, which means the efficacy of Gleevec is reduced. There are tests for these genetic changes, known as BCR-ABL mutations, but the tests are not standardised, their use is not fully understood by physicians, and so they give inconsistent results. Therefore a panel of European experts has put together recommendations aimed at rationalising the testing, and guiding physicians to when and how to do it effectively.

As part of the presentation, I saw the following slide presented at one meeting:

Map of all the amino acid substitutions in the Bcr-Abl KD identified in clinical samples from patients reported to be resistant to imatinib in published papers.

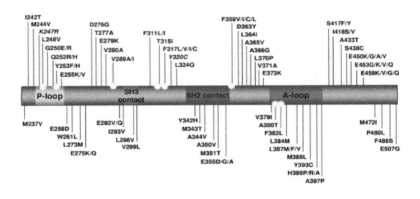

Simona Soverini et al. Blood 2011;118:1208-1215

Fig 3.16

The presenter then set about explaining it, in far too much detail. In the list of lost causes, that comes fairly high!

The problem

This is a classic case of confusing the paper with the presentation. I looked at the audience while the presenter was doing his best at trying to explain the slide, and I predict that the iPhone count was high, as many of them decided to check their emails. The slide is far too complicated to be explained in a presentation, particularly one where the audience were not experts in the gene mutation. They were haematologists who treat CML. Their WIFFM question was simply, 'What does this mean to the way I treat my patients?'

How to improve it

Firstly, be aware of the audience, how much they know, need to know, and can take in. Then, think about whether you need this slide at all. What is it telling them? Having heard the presenter, I wasn't sure, so I looked it up. The journal paper states:

"The list of amino acid substitutions detected in imatinib-resistant patients has steadily grown to include more than 90 different ones (**Figure 1**), although some are definitely more frequent than others. Different mutations have been shown to confer variable degrees of resistance to imatinib."

So this slide is an impressionistic one, showing the size and severity of the problem. Hardly anyone could talk us through it. However, it's impressive in the way it paints the picture of the problem. My suggestion is to keep the slide, but present it very differently. He might have said, *"To illustrate the size of the problem of resistance, I'm going to show you a complicated slide. I don't expect any of us to grasp every data point, but it does a good job to show what we are dealing with.*

[Reveal slide]. The resistance to imatinib can be identified by the amino acid substitutions. So far, more than 90 of these have been identified...and here there they are. Some are likely to make the patient more resistant than others, but all of these are problematic."

He could have then given us a brief overview of the meaning of the four coloured areas (green, blue, lilac and pink), told us where to find more information and then moved on.

Did you notice how my explanation of the situation followed the **And - But - Therefore** structure I introduced in the Storytelling section of the book? Here it is again, with highlighting:

Some people develop a type of blood cancer called Chronic Myeloid Leukemia (CML), **AND** are treated with drugs called Tyrosine Kinase Inhibitors (TKIs). The most common one is called imatinib, or Gleevec. **BUT** over time, they develop mutations in their genes, which means the efficacy of Gleevec is reduced. There are tests for these genetic changes, known as BCR-ABL mutations, but the tests are not standardised, their use is not fully understood by physicians, and so they give inconsistent results. **THEREFORE** a panel of European experts has put together recommendations aimed at rationalising the testing, and guiding physicians to when and how to do it effectively.

Statin slides

Background and Prior Work

Current statin guidelines emphasize the need to achieve
specific goals for LDLC to maximize clinical outcomes.

However, accumulating data indicates that statin therapy
has greatest efficacy in the presence of inflammation and
that statins reduce the inflammatory biomarker hsCRP
in a manner largely independent of LDLC.

Further, in both the PROVE IT – TIMI 22 and A to Z trials of
patients with acute coronary ischemia treated with statin
therapy, the best clinical outcomes occurred among those
who not only achieved LDLC < 70 mg/dL, but who also
achieved hsCRP levels < 2 mg/L. In both of these trials, even
greater clinical benefits accrued when hsCRP levels were

Fig 3.17

Background and Prior Work

These prior data are consistent with the understanding that
atherothrombosis is a disorder of both hyperlipidemia
and inflammation, and that statins have anti-inflammatory
as well as lipid-lowering properties.

Despite the consistency of these data, whether achieving
lower levels of hsCRP after initiation of statin therapy is
associated with improved clinical outcomes in a similar
manner to that associated with achieving lower levels
of LDLC remains highly controversial.

We prospectively tested this hypothesis in the large-scale
XYZ10 trial.

Fig 3.18

The problem

These are two introductory slides presented to cardiologists. They explain the background to a trial examining whether reducing high sensitivity C Reactive Protein, a marker of inflammation, in addition to reducing LDLC, the so-called 'bad cholesterol' would reduce cardiovascular events more than reducing LDLC alone.

The two slides commit one of the most common faults:

- This information presumably came from the publication abstract: The author has confused the paper and the publication.

- There is far too much text, making the slides cluttered and difficult to read for the audience

- The text contains full sentences. This makes it almost certain that the presenter will read the slides out, reducing his/her role to an audio track to the slides, rather than remaining as the dominant figure in the presentation.

- There's so much text on the first slide that the end of the sentence has disappeared, making it impossible to understand

- This amount of text will take too long to read out. The audience can read silently faster than the presenter can read aloud intelligibly. They will therefore have reached the end ahead of him/her. Many presenters realise this, so speed up to make it less obvious. This detracts from their authority.

How to improve them

Reduce the amount of text.

Use phrases not sentences. For example:

Do statins work best when inflammatory markers present?

Trials suggest greatest outcome benefit with biggest hsCRP reduction:

- PROVE IT – TIMI 22

- A to Z

Target reduction: <1 mg/l hsCRP

He could have put more information in the notes pages if they were going to form the basis of the handout.

This approach leaves the speaker to elaborate on what the slide shows, and sets the scene neatly and briefly. You then leave yourself with enough to say, to add to what's on the screen. You may start your talk like this:

"We all know that reducing LDLC, the so-called 'bad cholesterol', reduces someone's risk of having a cardiovascular event. And we know that statins reduce LDLC effectively, and that's why they are recommended for at-risk patients.

However, there is increasing evidence to suggest that statins also reduce inflammation, as indicated by a biomarker called hsCRP, or high sensitivity C-Reactive Protein. This protein is produced by the liver during inflammation, which has been associated with the presence of heart disease.

Statins can reduce this, as well as reducing LDLC...but what is less clear is what that means to outpatients with a higher than normal risk of a CV event? So the question we addressed was, 'Does reducing the level of hsCRP as well as LDLC, by statin therapy, reduce someone's chances of a CV event?' In this study, we aimed at reducing the hsCRP by 1 mg per litre."

HIV treatment

Conclusions

- In treatment-experienced patients, including those with NNRTI resistant virus, ABC125 was superior to placebo
  - 64% of patients achieved confirmed undetectable viral load (<50 copies/mL) with ABC125 + BR at Week 26
- Even in the absence of any other fully active background agents (PSS = 0), with ABC125, 53% of patients achieved undetectable (<50 copies/mL) viral load
  - response rates increased as more active agents were used in the BR
- Better responses were achieved in patients with higher CD4 cell counts and lower viral loads for both treatment arms
  - higher responses were apparent with ABC125 compared with placebo, for all categories of baseline viral load or CD4 cell count
- 11 ABC125 RAMs were identified
  - an increasing number of ABC125 RAMs was associated a decreasing response in both treatment arms
  - in the ABC125 group, the greatest added benefit was seen with <4 ABC125 RAMs
  - 79% of patients had <4 ABC125 RAMs
- ABC125 demonstrated significant activity and provides a new treatment option for patients with resistance to other NNRTIs

BR = background regimen; RAM = resistance-associated mutation;

Fig 3.19

The problem

This is the conclusion slide from a presentation about a new HIV treatment, which I've called ABC125. It was a type of drug known as an NNRTI, where resistance is known to develop over time, so the treatment becomes less effective. The slide was part of a presentation to HIV specialists, so the high number of acronyms, common in that therapy area, is not a problem. It's interesting that even then the authors found it necessary to explain two acronyms which they thought may not have been understood (BR and RAM).

The problem here is that there's too much text on the slide and it's too dense. As with the hsCRP example, the author has left herself with little or nothing to add to the words on the slide, so the slide becomes a teleprompter.

How to improve it

Split the conclusions across three slides, headed:

- Conclusions: Efficacy

- Conclusions: Resistance

- Summary

The summary slide should consist of one clear message about what it means to physicians and patients. It appears that this message is the final bullet point:

ABC124 demonstrated significant activity and provides a new treatment option for patients with resistance to other NNRTIs.

The HIV/AIDS area is full of heavy, data-driven slides and acronyms. Here's another confusing example from a presentation on the same topic:

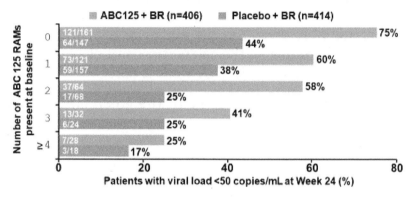

Fig 3.20

Resistance to HIV drugs is a big problem. RAMs are Resistance-Associated Mutations of HIV, ie bad news. The more you have, the less effective the treatment is likely to be.

The problem

This slide suffers from the same problems as the previous example: It's too dense. It's also confusing, because it contains too much data.

How to improve it

We don't need the numbers on the green lines – the percentages are sufficient information.

The chart is the wrong way up. I would have the zero mutations group at the bottom, building up to the four or more mutations at the top. This would also make it clear that those with the fewest mutations did best on the new drug.

The bullet points tell you what you want to know, ie that 86% of patients got great benefit and this was linked to the small number of RAMs. However, the bullets are themselves confusing. What does '86% of patients had fewer than 3 ABC125 RAMs' mean? Where's that data on the slide? When you present a figure in this way, people in the audience try and make the other figures add up to it. If the calculation isn't obvious, they'll tune out from your talk while they work it out.

I would change the colour of one of the green lines, so they are differentiated better. This also makes it easier to refer to them verbally.

Blood Pressure

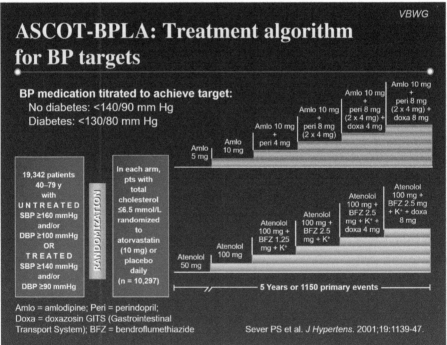

Fig 3.21

The problem

This is a typical slide I see presented at medical conferences. It was part of an introductory presentation about the blood pressure lowering arm of a huge trial called ASCOT, a landmark study in the prevention of CV events. The steps graphic on the right does a decent job of illustrating in an impressionistic manner how the treatments were stepped up as patients needed more medication to keep their blood pressure under control. However, the panels on the left make it too cluttered and difficult, not to say impossible, to read. As it stands, the drug and dosage details are too small to read from any distance.

Confusion like this takes the audience's minds off your talk, as they try to work out the correct facts.

How to improve it

The details on the panels on the left could have been put onto a separate slide, leaving more room for the steps. Alternatively, the steps on the right could have been summarised on the first slide, with the second slide being a 'zoomed in' view. Either of these suggestions would allow the text to be legible. The drug could have been differentiated by using different colours for the abbreviations.

Best Practice

Here are some good examples of medical data slides. They all contain very clear combinations of text and graphics. Although they relate to medical matters and clinical trials, the lessons are universal when applied to textual or graphical slides.

My first example is based on a classic piece of data from the Framingham Heart Study. This has followed residents of Framingham, Massachusetts since 1948 and is now on its third generation of participants. It has revealed many useful insights into heart disease based on diet, exercise and common medications such as aspirin.

One of the key findings was the way that modifiable risks of CV disease (obesity, smoking, high cholesterol, diabetes and high blood pressure) multiply, rather than add up. This means that two risk factors increase your risk of a CV event four-fold, rather than doubling it. So if you're obese and smoke, your risk of cardiovascular disease is four times as high as someone who only does one of those things. This is a complicated (and very important!) message to get across, but it was achieved by very thoughtful use of design and animation. The designers produced this slide, which 20 years later remains a model of best practice:

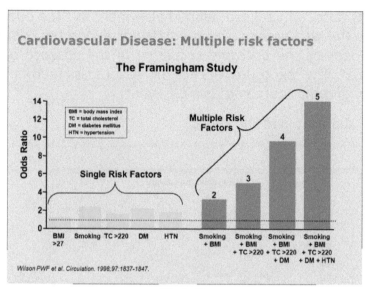

Fig 3.22

However, it was not just the design of the slide which was so impressive – it was the use of animation. So when it was presented, it came in three parts:

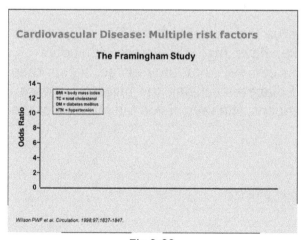

Fig 3.23

As with any data slide, it's important to first set the scene. The presenter does this by talking about the Framingham Study and introducing the risk factors for CV disease. She then points us to the odds ratio, which I see defined elsewhere as *"the odds that an outcome will occur given a particular exposure, compared to the odds of the outcome occurring in the absence of that exposure"*. The 'exposure' here is the various risk factors for CV disease, and the 'outcome' is a CV event.

Then she animates the slide:

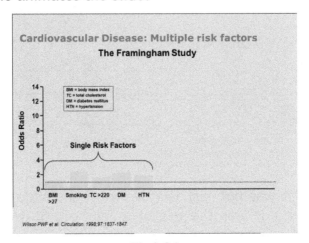

Fig 3.24

She shows us the increased odds of a CV event if you are obese, smoke, have high cholesterol, diabetes or high blood pressure. You can see that they all go higher than one, with smoking and diabetes causing the biggest increase in risk. But look what happens, she says, if you fall into two of the categories mentioned. :

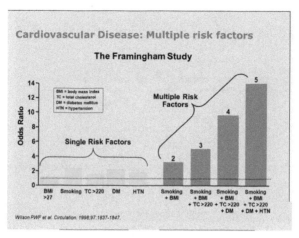

Fig 3.25

'The odds don't just add up…they multiply. So if you have all of these risk factors, you are 14 times more likely to have a CV event than if you don't have any.' That's the beauty of the Framingham Study – it's shown us this very important fact, illustrated here by a beautiful slide. As an example of slide design and animation to illustrate data, it's unsurpassed.

My next examples also concern CV risk. They come from a study called PLATO CABG. This compared a new drug, called ticagrelor, with an older drug, called clopidogrel, in patients with Acute Coronary Syndrome. Both drugs are anti-platelet agents, designed to prevent blood clots. Patients usually receive aspirin and clopidogrel, but there are drawbacks to this, as the background slide explained, particularly if they require further surgery. (NSTEMI and STEMI are different types of heart attack, and a CABG is a heart bypass, known as a Coronary Artery Bypass Graft. All these terms are very familiar to the audience).

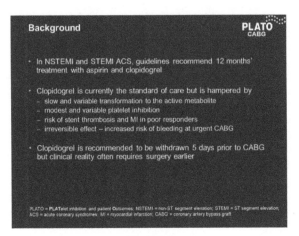

Fig 3.26

The key issue was that if patients need a bypass, and are on clopidogrel, they have to wait until the drug has washed out of their system. Having clearly outlined the background, the next slides described the objectives, and the patient flow:

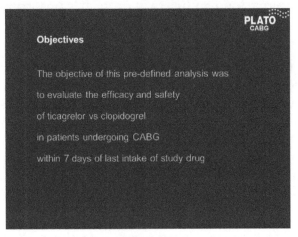

Figs 3.27

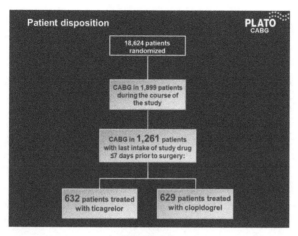

Figs 3.29

So far, so very clear. However, it's in the reporting of the results that the slide designers have excelled themselves. They've followed all the suggestions for dark background/light text, one message per slide, keeping text to a minimum and using the same format for the slides. Crucially, the scales and labels are clear, and the clopidogrel and ticagrelor colours are clearly differentiated. Here are some examples:

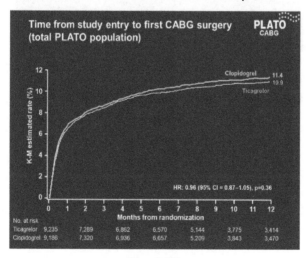

Figs 3.29

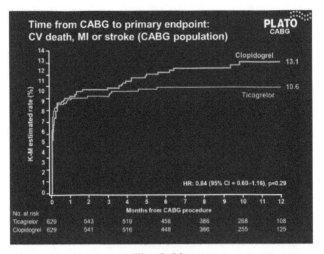

Figs 3.30

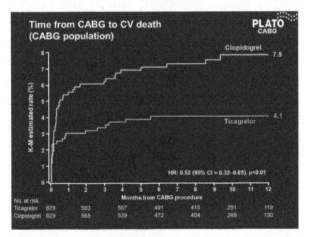

Figs 3.31

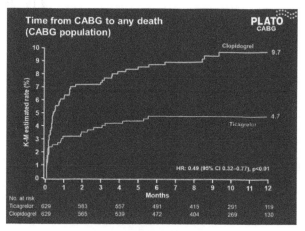

Figs 3.32

Bar chart example

I see a lot of bar charts presented. Very rarely are they as clear as these two. I love everything about them...the clarity of the titles, the use of colours, the clear explanatory keys.

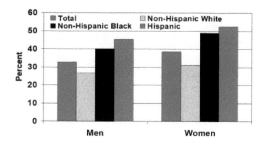

Narayan et al, JAMA, 2003

Figs 3.33

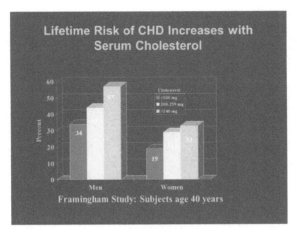

Figs 3.34

Here is another good example of PowerPoint being used to give an overall impression, rather than detailed information:

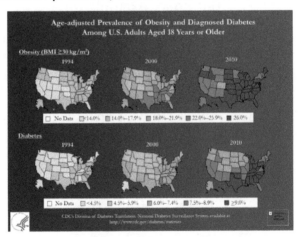

Fig 3.35

You can see clearly from this that the rates of obesity and diabetes have mirrored one another, and increased dramatically in the 16 years covered by the data. If someone wants to know more, the reference is there.

Part 3 - Summary

PowerPoint can be a real benefit if you use it properly

The slides are your visual aids, not vice versa

There are three main reasons for unclear slides:

- Inappropriate usage

- Muddled thinking

- Overestimating how much detail people can absorb

The published research paper and the presentation require different levels of detail

Just because you know it all does not mean you have to say it all

Follow the tips in this chapter to declutter your slides. In particular:

- Avoid full sentences

- Do not paste in tables and other graphics from clinical papers

- Use colours, arrows, circles and other graphic devices to aid clarity

- Split text across two or more slides if necessary...or reduce the amount

- Avoid fancy PowerPoint tricks that obscure the facts

THE LAST WORD

My aim in this book has been to encourage you to stop relying on PowerPoint slides and free your inner storyteller. I hope I've followed my own advice, and informed, engaged and inspired you to do that. The book is based on the techniques I have developed over many years as a storyteller and a trainer of storytellers. During that time I've met many people who have taken on my ideas, incorporated them into their own talks, improved them and made them their own. I love it when that happens.

However, there are others who will never be entirely comfortable with the concept of storytelling. There are a number of reasons: Some feel it's just not them. They have an analytical, possibly introverted personality and they're more comfortable with data and facts. I hope I've not given the impression that data and facts are not important, because I believe they are the basis for any talk, unless you've been hired as a stand-up comedian or after-dinner speaker. In the world of pharmaceuticals, science and medicine where I work regularly, facts and data trump everything else. My focus is on how you communicate that information.

I love the idea of stories being like a Trojan Horse, sneaking facts into the citadel of people's brains. If you're not comfortable with that, please don't try it. Remember, you need to be authentic, and if you're not, the audience will spot it. However, for you there is a halfway house: Stop reading slides, simplify your slides and narrative, have a clear aim, and good structure and an action point. If this applies to you, use The Grid method of planning a talk, and leave it at that. I hope that will improve your presentations.

A question I am often asked is 'Are you suggesting that I use storytelling techniques in every presentation?' My answer is that it depends on you, but that the approach I have advocated in this book will add impact to most of your talks. However, you have to decide how comfortable you are with the approach, and how it will be received by the audience. As so often, the word 'appropriate' is the key. In reality there are very few times when you can't use it to good effect. Mark Lanier, a lawyer in Houston, Texas, controversially used storytelling techniques known as 'Beyond Bullet Points' in a court case against the pharmaceutical giant Merck. He won a $253 million settlement for his client (though it was reduced on appeal). That example shows that, with the right planning, presentation and delivery, the techniques I've advocated here can be used in even the most formal settings.

I've introduced a lot of techniques in the book, and I don't expect you to use them all – at least not immediately. Start slowly with baby steps and reduce the chances of falling over. For example, try adding contrast to illustrate your case, and use the And...But...Therefore technique to explain a gap in the market or unmet need. You may not be comfortable using personal stories and creating memorable moments right now, but once you gain confidence in the techniques, I hope you're feel inspired to give them a try.

Finally, I hope that the many examples I've used have been a useful starting point for you. In practice, you can always produce your own, better ones. If you do produce them, and whether they're a triumph or disaster, please share your story with me. You can contact me on Twitter @JClionsden, find me on LinkedIn, or via my company website: www.lionsdencommunications.com

I wish you the best of luck in all your presentations.